Feeding Our FAITH with the GOSPELS

A Biblical Study of Jesus' Impact as Messiah

PETER PHIPPS

Author Credits: Author of 'Following Jesus through the Bible'

WestBow Press books may be ordered through booksellers or by contacting:

WestBow Press
A Division of Thomas Nelson & Zondervan
1663 Liberty Drive
Bloomington, IN 47403
www.westbowpress.com
1 (866) 928-1240

ISBN: 978-1-4908-5320-8 (sc)

Library of Congress Control Number: 2014917170

Printed in the United States of America.

WestBow Press rev. date: 9/29/2014

Contents

Acknowledgements

My first book, 'Following Jesus through the Bible', represented the first year's teaching of the Bible module at the Aberystwyth Academy of Christian Discipleship. This present book is a summary of the second year's course.

The forty or so regular members of this monthly class have been a great encouragement and working with the organising committee has been a joy. I am grateful for the friendship and support of Robin, Jean, Margaret, Hannah and Stuart.

I have tried to be honest with the material set before us in the four gospels, aiming to read them as their first readers would have read them. I am aware that it is so easy for anyone to lapse into a trend that ends up treating Jesus as little more than the servant of one or other of our ideological systems. Our reading of church history should show us how far we can stray from the original.

Scriptural quotations are from the NIV, and for ease of reading I have included the biblical references in the main body of the text. As with the previous book, it is best read in instalments, say a chapter a week. It is a study aid, designed to offer a working knowledge of the four gospels.

CHAPTER 1

The Authors and their Purpose

If we didn't have a New Testament and were entirely dependent on secular history, the information we would have about Jesus Christ would be very sparse and meagre. Roman historians such as Tacitus (AD 55-120) and Suetonius (AD 69-130) mentioned him rather incidentally and only when the Roman Empire was directly involved. Otherwise they were just not interested. Their writings do serve a useful purpose, however. Unsympathetic as they were to the claims, values and beliefs of the Christians, they do at least show that Jesus Christ was a real historical figure and one who exercised some considerable influence on his followers.

When Tacitus mentioned the fire that destroyed Rome in AD 64 for which the emperor Nero had blamed the Christians, he felt he needed to explain who those Christians were. He identified them as a sect that had originated from their founder leader Christ, a man who had suffered the ultimate penalty of death when Pontius Pilate had been the procurator of Judea in the reign of the emperor Tiberius. Tacitus tainted the members of the sect as those who were hated by the general public and the movement itself as a bad superstition which though initially checked had broken out again in Judea, and had even spread to Rome.

Suetonius, a younger contemporary of Tacitus, served as a court official under the emperor Hadrian. When he recorded the expulsion of the Christian Jews from Rome he described them as a group who had been a source of constant disturbance at the instigation of Christ.

Pliny the Younger was the Roman governor of Bithynia in Asia Minor. In AD 112 he wrote to the emperor Trajan to clarify what lawful action should be taken against the large number of those who were being accused of being Christians. He described them as a group that met regularly on a fixed day before it was light, when they sang a hymn to Christ as if he were a god, made their vows to abstain from fraud, theft, adultery and false witness, and then ate some food together.

These records by the Romans were enhanced by certain Jewish and Greek writers. The first century Jewish historian, Josephus, mentioned Jesus as a person in history as did some Jewish rabbinical writings that were put together in the Babylonian Talmud. And Lucian of Samosata, a second century Greek satirist, wrote that the early Christians worshipped the man who had been crucified. They lived by his laws, treated one another as brothers, and denied the gods of Greece.

This is all very well as far it goes. But our debt is to the writers of the New Testament whose work at the least stands as a bloc of ancient literature that sets out to describe and interpret the events surrounding the advent of one whom they present as no less a personage than the promised Messiah, the Son of God.

These writers have presented us with a fuller picture. They wrote down all that they considered was necessary for their readers to know.

The Story Summarised

The first four books of the New Testament record the significance, character, mission and achievement of Jesus of Nazareth as the Promised One.

The first three of these – Matthew, Mark and Luke – view his life from the same general standpoint and follow the same chronological pattern. They are therefore known collectively as the 'synoptic' gospels and any one of them can be used to supplement the other two. The fourth book – John – is completely different in form and arrangement. It is much more of a carefully argued theological case supported by biographical references to Jesus. For that reason it seems more profitable to study it separately.

From the three synoptic writers, we can discern seven distinct stages in the story of Jesus Christ.

1. It starts with the account of his birth and early years.
2. Then, when he was thirty, we have recorded the preparation for his public ministry – involving his herald, his baptism and temptation.
3. Jesus then promoted the message of his kingdom in Galilee in the north of the country.
4. Closely linked to this was a time of ministry in the northern regions outside Galilee.
5. This was followed by the long journey southwards to Jerusalem in Judea during which he continued to teach.
6. At Jerusalem his confrontation with the leaders of the Jewish religious establishment came to a head.
7. There he would be crucified, and after dying would rise again from death.

This is the order followed by Matthew, Mark and Luke. At some points there are striking similarities. For instance, the three of them cover the closing events at Jerusalem in roughly the same amount of detail (Matthew 21-28, Mark 11-16 and Luke 19-24). But there are obvious and significant differences too.

For example, whereas Matthew and Luke devoted their first two chapters to matters relating to the birth of Jesus, Mark doesn't mention it at all, devoting a greater percentage of his material to Jesus' destiny in Jerusalem. Matthew has a much longer section than the other two relating to Jesus' ministry in the north of the country (Galilee and the surrounding area), devoting three full chapters to the Sermon on the Mount alone. And Luke allocated nine chapters to his account of the journey to Jerusalem (Luke 10-18), and included a great deal of teaching Jesus gave on the way that is unique to his gospel.

The Authors

The cultural world into which Jesus was born was influenced by Jewish religion, Roman politics and the Greek language. In another context these could well have become insuperable obstacles, but not to the purpose of God in Jesus Christ. Jesus belonged to the human race as a whole. His appeal surmounted all barriers. It was therefore very appropriate that when he died the inscription above him on his cross describing him as King of the Jews was written in Hebrew, Latin and Greek. And it would appear that the writers of the first three gospels each targeted a particular strand of this wide audience.

Mark, or John Mark, was related to a leading figure in the Jerusalem church, Joseph nicknamed Barnabas (Colossians 4:10). He was at different times a support worker to the apostle Paul and a close associate of Peter (1 Peter 5:13). In later life he was with both Peter and Paul in Rome, and maybe wrote his gospel there. His work was the first to be written and is the shortest of the records. Both Matthew and Luke would make wide use of it. It has an uncomplicated storyline written from the standpoint of an eyewitness. It is quite possible that Mark himself witnessed some of the events he recorded, and it has been suggested he may even have been the young man who was almost apprehended when Jesus was arrested (Mark 14:51-52). What is more certain is that Peter was his source. The Aramaic phrases and vivid detail may be his. It can be argued that Mark's target audience were Romans. This would explain his use of several Latin phrases. It would also account for the fact that he limited his quotes from the Old Testament and completely omitted any record of Jesus' ancestry. Mark would have his readers see that Jesus as the Messiah was *God's anointed servant*, in harmony with Jesus' own words that 'the Son of Man did not come to be served, but to serve' (Mark 10:45). Jesus was pictured as constantly on the move, the phrase 'and immediately' occurring over forty times in an action packed ministry which included eighteen miracles. But Mark recorded only one of Jesus' discourses and only four of his parables.

Matthew, whom both Mark and Luke refer to as Levi, was a Jew who had worked as a tax collector for Herod Antipas and the Romans but gave it up to become one of Jesus' disciples and then one of his twelve apostles.

He was not a tunnel-vision nationalistic Jew. As well as Mark's gospel he used his own material and a resource of Jesus' sayings which was also used by Luke. He frequently quoted Old Testament prophecy to make his point that Jesus was its fulfilment. It seems reasonable to conclude that he was writing with Jews in mind. He presented Jesus as *his people's King.* His emphasis when Jesus was born was enshrined in the question of the visitors from the east: 'Where is the one who has been born king of the Jews?' (Matthew 2:2). He referred to Jesus several times as 'the Son of David' and documented extensive teaching about the Kingdom of heaven that Jesus proclaimed. So he included five of Jesus' discourses which were quite lengthy and several of his parables. He also prefaced his whole account with an ancestral line which was traced back to David through the royal line. Jews would have been interested in Matthew's gospel.

Luke was a physician, an associate of Paul and one of his most loyal friends (Acts 28:8-10, Colossians 4:14). He was a Gentile with a good command of classical Greek, and his work would therefore appeal to Greeks. He presented Messiah Jesus as *the world's Saviour.* At Jesus' birth Luke emphasised the announcement of the angels to the shepherd: 'Today in the town of David a Saviour has been born to you; he is Christ the Lord' (Luke 2:11). He mentioned the concept of grace eight times, the related words, 'saved', 'salvation' and 'Saviour' fourteen times, and the phrase 'tell glad tidings' ten times. He used words such as 'all flesh', 'all nations' and 'a light for the Gentiles'. It was Luke who recorded the Christian hymns spoken by Zachariah, Mary and Simeon as well as the parables of the prodigal son, the debtors, the Good Samaritan and the rich man and Lazarus.

The three authors each set their particular emphasis in their opening words.

The Prefaces

Mark 1:1, Matthew 1:1-17, Luke 1:1-4

Mark – the announcement of good news

Mark was to set something of a literary precedent, for before he put his pen to paper there was no genre of literature known as 'gospel'.

His opening sentence was a sort of title or an arresting announcement – 'The beginning of the gospel about Jesus Christ, the Son of God' (Mark 1:1). Though the word 'gospel' may be familiar to us, its meaning is much deeper than we might have thought at first sight. We might even know that the Greek word means good news or glad tidings. This is true, but it is not the whole story. In ancient times, both in the Jewish and Roman worlds, the word was used in a narrower and more technical way.

For example, in the Greek translation of the Old Testament known as the Septuagint it appears twice in the work bearing the name of the prophet Isaiah. The prophet had referred to the cities of Judah as the recipients of good news (Isaiah 40:9), but it was good news that contained a precise and particular message: 'Here is your God.' 'See, the Sovereign Lord comes with power, and his arm rules for him. See, his reward is with him and his recompense accompanies him' (Isaiah 40:9,10). The idea was repeated in Isaiah 52:7 – 'How beautiful on the mountains are the feet of those who bring good news, who proclaim peace, who bring good tidings, who proclaim salvation, who say to Zion, "Your God reigns."' From these verses we can see that the term 'gospel' was good news that specifically broadcast God's appearance on the scene as a King.

An ancient inscription from the Roman world of 9 BC also used the term. It concerned the emperor Augustus Caesar to the effect that he was the virtuous instrument of a higher Providence that had planned the best for humanity. The fact that wars had ceased and that order had been restored and maintained should be sufficient reason for all who came under Rome's government to regard him as a global benefactor and saviour. The birthday of the Emperor therefore had significance for the world as the beginning of the 'gospel' concerning him.

We get closer to understanding the meaning of the word as Mark used it, when we see that it was concerned with the particular news that a new king had ascended His throne to bring salvation and peace. So, in introducing Messiah the king, Mark deliberately chose the word 'gospel' as a word that both Jew and Gentile would know. The fortieth chapter of Isaiah influenced his choice. He knew it well, for he would quote its prophecy concerning the voice shouting in the wilderness to prepare the way of the Lord.

Messiah's coming was news, good news, even the best news. We must be clear about this. The gospels were written not as someone's good advice, comment or opinion, and not even as a complete biography. As a narrated story they stand as good news concerning an historical person, 'Jesus Christ, the Son of God.' Jesus was his human name that meant Saviour; Christ, the Greek equivalent for Messiah in Hebrew, was a title that meant the Anointed One, a status that was intended to be understood as divine. The promised coming of Yahweh was fulfilled in the coming of Jesus the Son of God, presented as the Saviour, Messiah and God incarnate. The focus of the gospels could not be any higher or worthier. But as with all news, it is meant to be read, understood, accepted and believed.

Matthew – an official identification (the genealogy)

By contrast, Matthew began his account with a list of Jesus' ancestors (Matthew 1:1-17) which included two identifying marks that would later become significant New Testament pegs for spiritual truth: as 'the Son of David' Jesus was linked to the royal Messianic line of Judah, and as 'the son of Abraham' he would be the channel of God's blessing to the Gentiles. Luke also included a family tree, but his list of names differed from Matthew's. The two lists were identical from Abraham to David, but at that point Matthew traced the line of descent to Jesus through David's son King Solomon, whereas Luke followed it through Nathan, an older son of David. It has long been accepted that Luke recorded the family tree of Mary (from Nathan), and that Matthew recorded the ancestry of Joseph (from Solomon). Solomon's was the recognised royal line and Nathan's a legal line which could present a valid claim if there was no reigning royalty in the line of Solomon.

In Matthew's record there is a noticeable change of form in verse 16 from 'the father of' to 'the husband of', which supports his subsequent account of the virgin birth of Jesus. Matthew did not say that Joseph was the father of Jesus, but that he was 'the husband of Mary, of whom was born Jesus, who is called Christ.' By adoption Joseph became the legal father of Jesus in the royal line but was not his biological father. This detail becomes quite a crucial one when we read that one of the kings of Judah in Solomon's line to Joseph, King Jeconiah (Matthew 1:11), had been placed under an official ban which listed him as 'childless' as far as the succession was concerned, and excluded all of his biological descendants from the throne (Jeremiah 22:30). Jesus remained unaffected by this ban, but as a legally adopted son of Joseph could take his place in the royal line. He also had an independent legal claim through his mother, which by-passed the ban on Jeconiah's descendants.

Unusually for Jewish genealogies, Matthew included the names of four women, and even more strangely they were all Gentile women – Tamar, Rahab (mother of Boaz), Ruth (wife of Boaz and great grandmother of David), and Bathsheba (referred to as the one who 'had been Uriah's wife'). In Matthew's appeal to Jews, therefore, alongside his identification of Jesus as the son of David and son of Abraham he started his record with a very strong hint of Jesus' universal interest.

Luke – a reference point for instruction

As a writer, Luke claimed the role of a careful researcher of oral and written sources. He said that he had examined several documents containing eyewitness accounts. In writing to a dignitary named Theophilus, who had received a course of Christian teaching, Luke indicated the two ways in which he treated the events of Jesus' life: on the one hand he saw them as fulfilling all the Old Testament promises that had enshrined God's long term commitment to his people, and on the other hand they constituted a foundation for the teaching of all new disciples. In the coming of Jesus as the Messiah, Luke stressed that God's promises were honoured, and it was on that basis that the themes of salvation, redemption and forgiveness of sins through Jesus featured strongly as major elements in his writing.

It is Luke's record that starts the story of Messiah at its earliest point with his account of some rather unique announcements that were given by angels. On first reading, we who belong to a different culture, place and time may wonder how we should take this. But we are to remember that Luke was the man who claimed to be a clear-headed, feet-on-the-ground historian who was employing a valid method of research. And it was with no apology, explanation or embarrassment that he recorded the role that the angelic community played in the opening scenario.

For this reason, it is profitable for us at the outset to analyse and assess our own grasp of matters which Luke and the other New Testament writers accepted as realities. For in addition to their belief in the activity of angels, they also recorded the confrontation that Jesus had with demons. It would help our understanding immensely if we addressed this whole issue at the start, and as we do so to free ourselves from all sorts of cluttering influences – whether of familiarity, sentimentalism, cynicism or naivety.

We live in time and space, and our five senses make us conscious of the world around us. We are at ease with this. But it soon becomes obvious that reality cannot be reduced to that level of awareness that is measurable by mere human sight or hearing. For example, the human mind exists as a reality somewhere in the human brain, but it is not subject to the same conditions that even apply to the brain. The brain has physical properties like shape, size, weight and colour. The mind does not. But its invisibility is no argument against its existence.

God is described as essentially spirit – a mode of reality that is as different from matter as the flame is from the candle. It may take time for us human mortals to get our minds around the concept of an uncreated God who is intangible spirit and yet a person. But many of us have done so; and once we have, it is a much shorter step to accept the notion of created spirit beings. In fact, we as earthly human beings, made in God's image, are not just social animals with a sharpened spiritual dimension. We are personal spirit beings that inhabit a body of flesh, bone and blood. Our five physical senses give us world awareness. Memory and reason feed our appreciation of visual, aural and tactile art. We can think abstractly. Our consciences provide a guide to ethical and moral issues. Unhurried reflection will reveal the wonder of how biological, intellectual, psychological and spiritual factors interact in our makeup.

The Bible informs us that there is a large heavenly community of spirit beings who do not have the limitations of human bodies. These angels form a vast community who have been created directly by God, who do not reproduce and who do not die – individuals in the strictest of senses (Luke 20:35,36). They fulfil a triple role as ardent worshippers of almighty God (Isaiah 6, Revelation 4), submissive learners of his purposes (1 Peter 1:12, Ephesians 3:10) and obedient servants of his will (Hebrews 1:7,14). The Bible writers unquestioningly accept their existence so that they even refer to them in the most incidental of ways (1 Corinthians 4:9, 1 Timothy 5:21, Hebrews 12:22).

Demons or evil spirits, on the other hand, are presented as fallen angels who have refused to worship God and who attack the purpose of God wherever their leader Satan chooses. Instead of directing worship toward God, Satan himself yearns to be worshipped – he said as much to our Lord during his wilderness temptation. Some of the fallen angels have already been judged; others are still active in the world.

It should therefore come as no surprise to us that surrounding the whole earthly life and ministry of Jesus the Messiah, angels were said to be active in glad support and ready service. Jesus himself said that they joyfully celebrated the success of his mission to get sinners to repent (Luke 15:7,10). Angelic activity started with Gabriel's announcement of the birth of John as Messiah's herald, and his appearing to Mary (Luke 1:11-19, Luke 1:26-35). In a dream, an angel would assure Joseph and guide him to do the right thing (Matthew 1:20). A group of angels celebrated Jesus' actual birth (Luke 2:9, Hebrews 1:6). They supported him after the temptation (Mark 1:13) and in the garden of Gethsemane (Luke 22:43). They were on standby at the crucifixion (Matt.26:53), announced his resurrection (Mat 28:2,5), were there at the ascension (Acts 1:10) and will attend his return (Matthew 13:41, 16:27, 24:31, 1 Thessalonians 4:16).

Equally, Jesus attracted the attention of the powers of darkness. Evil spirits gathered to resist and oppose him. They saw him as a threat because his mission was to deliver human beings from every dark spiritual power. Yes, the ministry of Jesus would address the self-imposed slavery that resulted from human beings' personal sin and guilt, but it was also going to impact folk who in one way or another were tempted, oppressed, possessed and deceived by the spiritual powers of darkness.

The apostle Paul summed up the Messianic mission when he recounted his personal story to King Herod Agrippa. He told how

Messiah Jesus had sent him to both Jews and Gentiles, having authorised him with the task of spiritual enlightenment and deliverance. People's eyes would be opened and their faith activated as they were turned from darkness to light and delivered from the power of Satan to find in God forgiveness of sins and a place among his chosen people (Acts 26:18). Paul was keenly conscious right throughout his life of the intense struggle that Messiah's people would engage in with these wicked spiritual forces from the unseen world which he also described as the 'rulers', 'authorities' and 'powers of this dark world' (Ephesians 6:12).

It was over these very same powers that Messiah would visibly triumph on every occasion, culminating in his crucifixion and resurrection when they were viewed by Paul as captives in Messiah's victory procession. 'Having disarmed the powers and authorities, he made a public spectacle of them, triumphing over them by the cross' (Colossians 2:15). One of the purposes of his death was to 'destroy him who holds the power of death – that is, the devil – and free those who all their lives were held in slavery by their fear of death' (Hebrews 2:14,15). It was successful. For in the lives of his disciples, that ultimate fear would be replaced with a conscious awareness of the love of God. Paul could say, 'I am convinced that neither death nor life, neither angels nor demons … will be able to separate us from the love of God that is in Christ Jesus our Lord (Romans 8:38,39).

This is enough Biblical evidence to demonstrate that the mention of angels and demons was not due to any flight of fancy by authors with vivid imaginations. A real spiritual war existed which meant that life was not easy for Jesus. He was the Truth, and Satan was the father of lies.

Whenever angels and demons are mentioned, therefore, I trust we will take it seriously and resist the temptation to place the record in the category of fairy tale or myth.

CHAPTER 2

Messiah's Arrival

When the United States was attacked at Pearl Harbour on December 7, 1941, America became directly involved in World War II. The British Prime Minister, Winston Churchill, who had always believed that the great strength of America was crucial to the outcome of the war, expressed his assurance of ultimate victory for the allies in a memorable statement. He said that on hearing this news he 'went to bed and slept the sleep of the saved and thankful.' There was hope now.

The same could be said of the news of Messiah's arrival. Hope would replace a host of other emotions for those who were waiting for Messiah to come. It was a unique and crucial event. And as such, it would be marked by several signs of the supernatural that never would be repeated.

For instance, we will read of individuals who were personally prepared by the Holy Spirit, the visitation of angels to specially chosen folk, the fulfilment of Old Testament prophecy and the divine ordering of events and dreams. The three writers would have been dismayed if they had suspected their words would ever be treated as fictional make believe. They were not writing a fantasy. The Holy Spirit, the third person of the Trinity, was and is a reality. Angels, spirit beings directly created by God for his praise and service, were and are a reality. Fulfilled

Scripture was and is a reality. If this was the coming of no less a personage than God's Messiah, the Son of God, it was the most extraordinary and exceptional of all occasions. And the sane and balanced way in which the story is presented by men of integrity should carry weight with all who read it. Nothing like this is produced today. It is not required. Messiah has come.

Angelic announcements

The angelic message to Zachariah about John
Luke 1:5-23

God's plan was initially divulged to a couple of senior citizens who as spiritually prepared people had been praying. Both Elizabeth and Zachariah were upright and God fearing. They had prayed for what they considered would be good for them, but in their prayers they got closer than they had ever expected to God's great purpose as his agenda was revealed to them.

This programme of his was not a puzzle for them to solve, or a code they had to decipher. It did not require them to accumulate enough evidence to take some course of action. It was just a plain straightforward announcement of information that was meant to be believed.

When the angel Gabriel first spoke to Zachariah he didn't ramble or ad lib. He got straight to each point. A boy would be born as the answer to their prayers. He was to be named John (which means something like 'God is a gracious Giver'). He would be a joy to them and many others, but of far greater significance he would be 'great in the sight of the Lord' (verse 15). After all, it was God's estimation that counted.

This assessment of John was subsequently confirmed by Jesus in Matthew 11:11, when he said, 'Among those born of women there has not risen anyone greater than John the Baptist.' He was not a reed swayed by the wind like those who tried to please popular opinion, and because he did not have a luxurious lifestyle to maintain, he depended on no one (Matthew 11:7,8). His abstention from wine and fermented drink, a feature of the Old Testament Nazirite (Numbers 6:2-4), was a sign that he was separated to God's work and indicated that he was a channel for the power of the Holy Spirit. He would be filled with the Spirit from his birth (verse 15). He would speak and act 'in the spirit and the power of Elijah' (verse 17). He would bring back the wanderer, and prepare the people for the Messiah. Wow!

But cautious Zachariah, slow on the uptake, expressed some misgivings. How could he be sure of any of this? Gabriel, amazed, patiently explained. He who had stood to attention before the living, all powerful and glorious God had been sent by Him to tell the good news! And what did he see before him? A sluggish heart was showing signs of sheer unbelief. All right, then. Some discipline and proof was called for. Zachariah's unwillingness to respond to God's agenda would leave him unable to speak. He wouldn't have the chance to spread faithless words or even useful words. He would not be able to pray aloud or witness. Then Gabriel said 'Goodbye' and was gone.

The angelic message to Mary about Jesus
Luke 1:26-38

The story continued with the experience of the young virgin, Mary, who became one of Luke's primary sources as he made it his business to research his theme. Her story establishes principles that were directly related to the nature of faith – matters such as her personal commitment to God, spiritual fellowship and joyful worship.

The angel brought Mary a heavenly message – which, by contrast with Zachariah, she believed and received. Twice the angel spoke of God's grace – 'Greetings, you who are highly favoured! The Lord is with you' (verse 28); 'You have found favour with God' (verse 30). God was personally interested in her! He had abundantly endowed her with the grace she needed for her role. She listened, and came to realise that God had a great plan for her life. She was to be the channel through whom Messiah would come to earth in the flesh. Her son, to be named Jesus, would be the great one, the Son of the Most High and true heir of David's throne who would reign forever. Up until that moment, hers had been a quiet and unspectacular existence governed by the expectations of her time and status. But now she had been given an unprecedented and unrepeatable task and told that someone else was in charge. God lifted her out of the anonymous sphere of the humdrum and predictable world of routine decisions. Her life was now much more than existence. It was injected with spiritual meaning and significance. That at least was the plan which she could either reject or serve.

In the course of this heavenly dialogue, she learned that God could accomplish all of this his way – it was not down to human contrivance, but would be a supernatural and miraculous result of the work of the Holy Spirit. This element has often been downplayed in religious quarters and even given the status of myth. But if it is an invented story, then it is not true; and if it is not true, it has to be called an elaborate lie which calls into question the characters of Joseph, Mary and Luke. There are many of us still who are not prepared to do this. The alternative is that the virginal conception of Jesus was the miraculous work of the Holy Spirit. And Mary, realising this very same point, simply accepted the requirements of God through the angel without question or reservation. She believed that what the Lord had said to her would happen. From that moment on Mary's day-to-day life was ruled by her commitment to what she knew God wanted to do in and through her. 'I am the Lord's servant. May it be to me as you have said' (verse 38). Her acceptance meant that the Holy Spirit would come directly upon her, and the power of the Most High would overshadow her (verse 35).

Again, this has never been duplicated and never will be.

Of course, Mary must have known that for her to say 'Yes' to God, and follow God's way would mean that tongues would start to wag, and her reputation as a respectable Jewish virgin would be called into question by evil men who did not know the ways or the power of God. The old man Simeon would later tell her that a sword would pierce her soul (Luke 2:35). Her spiritual privilege involved a price – it was the cost of her discipleship.

Fellowship between Mary and Elizabeth
Luke 1:39-56

Mary was in need of understanding and support. But where could she find it? The angel Gabriel had given her a clear hint: 'Elizabeth your relative is going to have a child in her old age, and she who was said to be barren is in her sixth month. For nothing is impossible with God' (verses 36,37). The suggestion was that she would get spiritual strength in fellowship with Elizabeth. Fellowship is the sharing and enjoyment of what is held in common. It involves giving and receiving, speaking and listening. In this case, it was the sharing of the same sort of spiritual experience. God was performing heaven's work on earth, and both of these women were simply his willing and co-operative servants in his great plan. They could both share with each other what God had said and what God had started to do. They did not need to spend their time together in inventive imagination or philosophical speculation.

On the one hand, this spiritual fellowship transcended all artificial human barriers. It was not dependent on a common age group, social strata or religious status. Elizabeth was old, Mary still young. Elizabeth lived in the more reputable south of the country, while Mary was from rough-and-ready Galilee. Elizabeth was married; Mary was still single. Elizabeth was married to a priest; Mary was engaged to the village carpenter of Nazareth. None of these differences mattered however if the fellowship was created by the Holy Spirit.

On the other hand, because spiritual fellowship was related to this unique experience it was bound to be limited. It was not a clever human invention. Its origin was God. And the experience shared was intensely personal, private and internal. It would have been wrecked if it had been publicly paraded or widened to those who were strangers to God's ways. Folk would have wanted to analyse it, question it, dissect it, quibble about it and correct it. Elizabeth knew for herself the miracle of life in her womb and Mary still a virgin had been told that she would give birth to the Son of God. Both were moving in the realm of the sovereignty of God, a realm in which nothing was impossible. Elizabeth was not just Mary's sympathetic and understanding friend, but possessed real discernment and genuine spiritual recognition – so that when Mary arrived at her home, she recognised her as the future mother of her Lord, and her own unborn baby leapt in her womb. At this stage, not even those who were closest to them, Zachariah and Joseph, were ready for any of this, or could cope with it; they could not yet enter into the thrilling pleasure that dominated the two women. The angel still had a lot of work to do on those two men. Simeon and Anna, however, would have understood – they were the ones waiting in the Spirit for the ancient promise to be fulfilled; their hearts were tuned aright.

Elizabeth, still amazed that she herself had been so favoured by God, had a word of blessing for Mary. It was encouragement to go on believing – for God would accomplish what he promised. And so, Mary, her faith and joy fed by fellowship with Elizabeth, was equipped to face up to the future psychological and social strain awaiting her. She would shortly return to her own house, while Elizabeth would get on with the business of mothering John.

Mary's hymn of worship
Luke 1:46-55

Mary too was amazed that she had been favoured by God, and expressed it in what subsequently became one of the early Christian songs. Her prayer, like that of Hannah (1 Samuel 2:1-10), reflected her experience of a new revelation of God, and as she rejoiced in the implications of it she therefore breathed a spirit of composed rapture. A powerful spiritual element ran through her life, one of joy in the Lord her God, the Mighty One, the Holy One, the Merciful One, the Provider and the Satisfier.

She started by magnifying God as great. She saw that as the Mighty One he had power residing within him which became an awesome display of strength whenever he chose to exert any pressure. As the Holy One, both in name and nature, she saw him as separate and different, and therefore wholesome and uncontaminated. This God she knew was also merciful. It had been seen in his activity as he had performed mighty deeds. It was God who made the difference between progress and confusion, hunger and satisfaction, fruitfulness and uselessness. It was he who 'scattered the proud' but 'lifted up the humble'; it was he who would send away empty the self-sufficient rich but fill the hungry with good things.

Mary was being theological – but not coldly so. She contemplated God as *her* personal and mighty Saviour who had done great things for *her*. She had received the grace of God, and so she felt moved in her inner being to glorify her Lord and rejoice in God her Saviour. It was heartfelt. She rejoiced that this mercy and grace worked for the humble who feared God, for she was but the bride of a carpenter. And her soul danced at the thought that God had graciously and singularly blessed her. From that moment onwards all generations would recognise her blessing – happiness indeed. All that was happening could be traced back to God's promise to Abraham and his descendants. It was all anchored there. And God had been faithful. This wonderful hymn is a model of devotional theology.

The birth of John the Baptist
Luke 1:57-80

Heaven's messianic agenda started to materialise on earth as Elizabeth's boy was born and was welcomed into the world by family, friends and neighbours who shared the mother's joy. At his circumcision event a week later, these well-meaning folk nevertheless attempted to modify God's agenda in the interests of family tradition. Why name him John? The infant should at least carry the name of his father. They did not know that this issue was a sort of test God had set for Zachariah. The only thing that God had required him to do was to name his son John. God's plan would proceed with or without his consent. But if he was to get his speech back all he had to do was personally recognise that this was heaven's agenda. He had learned his lesson. It was no trivial issue for him. The priest radically adjusted his own ideas and submitted to God's. The agenda was followed. Elizabeth spoke up, 'He is to be called John.' Zachariah, still communicating with sign language and writing tablet, agreed. And the first thing he did with his restored speech was to praise God. The news understandably spread through Judea. Folk were intrigued as to what was going to happen. What was this boy going to become? They perceived the hand of God in all this.

Zachariah's hymn
Luke 1:68-79

Just like his wife, Zachariah was now filled with the Holy Spirit. But what he said first was not about little John, but about the Messiah who as yet was unborn. In faith he praised the Lord, the God of Israel, who had come to liberate his people with the provision of the Saviour from David's line. This he saw as the highest theme of history and the fulfilment of all the prophetic promises – especially the patriarchal covenant traceable to Abraham. Thinking in the thoughts and language of the spiritual Jewish remnant, he linked the spiritual qualities of serving God in holiness and righteousness to rescue from physical oppressors.

But turning then to his son, Zachariah recognised him as the future prophet of the Most High God. He would precede the Lord as his herald, speaking of such eternal values as the mercy of God that brought a salvation that was to be understood in terms of the forgiveness of sins. The coming of Messiah was like the rising of the sun, spelling heavenly light for those living in the dark shadow of death, and personal guidance for those treading the path of peace. He was the Light of salvation.

After Zachariah and Elizabeth died, John pursued his destiny by resorting to the desert hills near Hebron, while other related significant developments were taking place in Nazareth.

The birth and childhood of Jesus
Matthew 1:18–2:23, Luke 2

It is Messiah who now takes centre stage. Two of the gospel writers give us details of his birth and infancy, Matthew from Joseph's viewpoint and Luke from Mary's. Both writers preserve a sense of awe, reverence and mystery alongside the element of reality. But without any apology, they quite unashamedly took the position that this Jesus as the Messiah was a miraculous and divine provision. They emphasised the way that God the Holy Spirit worked in the whole proceedings. They explained how all the angelic announcements and activity had gained the attention and cooperation of the men and women who had to be involved. And they placed the whole event in the context of the many Old Testament Scriptures that they saw being fulfilled.

The angel's message to Joseph
Matthew 1:18-25

Joseph and Mary were betrothed to each other. The Jews considered betrothal or engagement to be a solemn covenant that could be ended only by a formal divorce. It was therefore not to be lightly embarked upon. The betrothed couple were referred to as 'husband' and 'wife' and any sexual unfaithfulness constituted a breach of contract. It was treated as adultery.

Mary's pregnant condition could not be concealed indefinitely and when it became obvious it posed a major problem for Joseph, who as an upright man not only wanted to do the right thing but also the kind thing. So he decided it was right not to go ahead with the marriage, but in compassion for Mary he wanted to end the contract in as discreet a way as possible. The whole issue was playing on his mind one night as he went off to sleep. In a dream an angelic word of reassurance resolved his dilemma. In brief, he was to have no qualms about proceeding with the marriage. Mary had not been unfaithful to him. Her pregnancy was caused by the Holy Spirit as a special one off event to ensure the arrival of the one who would save his people from their sins.

It is this sort of statement that stops us in our tracks. What are we to make of it? But we need to be clear as to the real point here. The gospel account of the virgin birth of Jesus is directly linked to the apostles' assertion of his pre-existence. This is the more difficult concept to take in. But if we accept the proposition that Jesus as the Son of God lived before he was born then the virgin birth ceases to be the primary problem. And this is precisely what the New Testament teaches. Paul and John made very clear statements about the matter.

Paul said that the strongest demonstration of Jesus' grace lay in the fact that though once rich he made himself poor (2 Corinthians 8:9); he always had the nature of God, but instead of holding on tightly to his privileges he took the place of a servant and became a human being (Philippians 2:6-8); as the Son of God he existed before all things (Colossians 1:17).

John too had no doubts. Jesus as the Word existed with God 'in the beginning'; and it was this same being, the agent of creation and the source of life, who lived among us as a human being (John 1:14); he had shared the glory of God before the world was made (John 17:5).

That is the core issue. Viewed in this light, if the divine Son of God was becoming man in a real incarnation, then nothing less than a supernatural birth was called for. And Matthew's testimony was indeed that God sent his Son into the world through the two agents of a human mother and the Holy Spirit, so that Jesus Christ was both human and divine, the man who is God. Matthew's conclusion, backed by the OT scriptures, was that the virgin's son would be called 'Immanuel' meaning 'God with us.' Jesus was being displayed as the God of salvation – God in human flesh delivering his people. Theological and physical matters were bound up together.

So Joseph would marry Mary, but they would have no sexual intimacy until after the birth of Jesus.

The circumstances of Jesus' birth
Luke 2:1-7

The policy of the Roman Emperor Augustus introduced a series of provincial censuses which were carried out every fourteen years, and which continued for several decades after his death. One of these is mentioned by Luke in Acts 5:37 as a reference point relating to the emergence of some agitator named Judas the Galilean. It was the census before that which was the one associated with the birth of Jesus. By coincidence, the governor of Syria at the time of both censuses was Quirinius who apparently served two separate terms in that office. Luke is still maligned in some quarters today, but papyri and inscriptions habitually vindicate his references to historical events.

Enrolment was by household at the town where the family's register was kept. Consequently, Joseph travelled from Nazareth in Galilee to Bethlehem in Judea with Mary accompanying him. It was at Bethlehem that she gave birth. The inn or lodging-house was full, so she had to make do and be resourceful. She wrapped the new born in strips of cloth and laid him in a stall which was either in a cave or in a place connected with the inn.

The shepherds
Luke 2:8-20

Shepherding was a lowly occupation, and shepherds lived a hard life. They were certainly not the social elite of the day. If Luke's aim had been to invent an effective piece of propaganda, what was he doing having shepherds to be the agents for the news? It is written as it is because this is the way it happened.

These particular shepherds were on duty in the fields near Bethlehem where flocks reserved for temple sacrifice were kept throughout the year. They would take turns to watch for thieves and predatory animals. That night, these ordinary folk were privileged to see the heavenly messenger and the glory of God – and be the first to receive the good news which Christians rejoice in still.

Today we have got used to media news which if it is unexpected is gloomy or otherwise is predictably dull. What these shepherds were to hear was neither gloomy nor dull, but news that was infused with great joy and that was relevant for all. It had no sting in the tail or any unwelcome flip side. It was good news indeed. The shepherds were initially afraid, true, but this was a common reaction to the supernatural. The angelic appearance was intended to dispel fear. And their fear did indeed evaporate with their acceptance of the joyful message of a Saviour's birth, and the availability of salvation for all.

The people under Rome's rule had been taught to call the emperor 'Saviour', and so folk were familiar with the term. Many Jews were looking for a political leader, while others were hoping for a saviour from sickness and physical hardship. God's agenda would prove to be so different. But at this point, the details could wait. The shepherds were told of the significance of this Saviour. He was the Anointed Messiah and Lord. He was both the theme of heaven's praise and the secret of earth's peace. For it was at the mention of his status that a great company of angels appeared and gave glory to God in the highest, and proclaimed peace to all men on whom his favour rested. *Pax Romana* could offer a tranquillity that was externally enforced, but the angelic chorus proclaimed a profound and permanent peace of mind and soul.

The shepherds' response to the news was a combination of faith, witness and praise. After the angels disappeared, they discussed the message urgently and resolved to test the word from heaven. There was no human factor involved in it; but if they found the signs as given by the angel they would be reassured as to the rest of the message. When they therefore found the baby lying in the manger, which verified the angel's words, they spread what they had been told about him, probably starting at the inn and then those they met on their return. They glorified and praised God. It had been no coincidence. They were the first to see the Saviour, the Messiah, the Lord, a baby not yet a day old who was even then the embodiment of salvation.

And the reason the shepherds would have given to Mary to explain their sudden visit would have been a tremendous reassurance to her. Political events had dictated that she was miles away from family and home, surrounded by strangers, with no hotel room and having to improvise with long strips of cloth and a manger for a crib. Who else could have known what she had known all along? But these shepherds knew. They spoke of a newly born baby, a manger and strips of cloth. They said they were looking for the Saviour because angels had given them these details of the birth as a sign. Angels! They were not to know that Mary had seen Gabriel nine months earlier. No wonder Mary treasured their story. It was independent evidence to her that God was in control and had been all along.

Simeon and Anna at the temple
Luke 2:21-38

Named as Jesus at his circumcision, probably at Bethlehem, Joseph and Mary later presented him to the Lord in accordance with the law. At the temple in Jerusalem, two aged people, Simeon and Anna, gave thanks separately for the infant whom they also discerned as the essence of salvation and redemption. In Simeon's case, here was a man who was spiritually alert because the Holy Spirit was with him, had told him he would live to see the Messiah and had prompted him at the right moment to go to the temple courts. Simeon therefore had only one thing on his mind when before him stood this young family. Was it just a coincidence? No. Simeon took Jesus in his arms and praised God. He could die now, because with his own eyes he had seen the incarnation of God's salvation. Here was the prepared gift for all people. Here was light for the Gentiles in the dark. Here was the glory of God's people Israel.

Like the words of the shepherds, these words of Simeon constituted assurance for Mary and Joseph. They were amazed. He could only have known what he did by divine revelation. Then Simeon gave them a blessing and addressed Mary seriously. The child, chosen by God, was also a sign from God. He would spell destruction as well as salvation for many would speak against him and deny the good news. Sorrow would break Mary's heart like a sharp sword. Mary's spiritual privilege involved an earthly cost. But the words of a Spirit filled man could not be treated lightly. It is quite possible that Simeon had already received a revelation from the Holy Spirit about the crucifixion.

The prophet Anna at the age of eighty four was another senior citizen of the believing Messianic community. She was already known as a woman of worship, prayer and fasting. To this she added thankfulness to God for Jesus and testimony about Jesus to all the spiritually receptive folk who were longing for redemption. Here was the gift of God's Messiah, God's Salvation, the Light of the Nations, the Glory of His People and the one to set them free.

Visit of the magi
Matthew 2:1-12

A little while later, and in a different context, wise men crowned their own enquiring search for Messiah by presenting him with their gifts and offering their worship. These 'magi' were people of contemplation, probably priest-sages from Arabia. They explained their visit to Jerusalem as a search for the one who was born as king of the Jews. They said they had observed his star when it first appeared in the sky. Their expectation of the coming of a kingly figure had probably built up as they worked through books of Jewish tradition, where they would have read for example that the star of the Messiah would shine forth from the east for fifteen days and if it was prolonged it would be for the good of Israel. They were probably also aware of Balaam's prophecy that a star would come out of Jacob and a sceptre rise out of Israel (Numbers 24:17).

We know that the night sky can exhibit different kinds of phenomena. And several attempts at explanations have been attempted, ranging from Kepler's observation of planetary conjunction every eight hundred years to the trajectory of a comet. The theories are interesting, and some are compelling; but the point that the magi made was that the rising star had aroused their attention, and spoke to them of the Messiah's appearing.

Using their common sense they travelled to the obvious place – Jerusalem. But though it was the obvious place, it was not the right place. Through such unusual agencies as Herod the Great, the chief priests and teachers of the law, God gave them the greater light of Messianic prophecy. Scripture had pinpointed the birthplace of Messiah as Bethlehem, where King David's family lived (Micah 5:2). And so, departing from Jerusalem, God once again gave them the guidance of the star.

The story culminated in their worship of the king which was purposeful and deliberate, joyful, focussed, discriminatory and costly. In that house, a child took precedence in their minds as well as in Matthew's record. They presented him with gifts appropriate for a king – gold, incense and myrrh. The contrast was staggering. Into a simple if not poor situation came precious metals, perfumes and spices. Then they returned home without reporting back to Herod.

In guiding them God had used Jewish literature, the words of a false prophet, a star in the sky, a tyrannical despot, the detached religious world and a dream. These all served God's purpose.

The stay in Egypt and return to Galilee
Matthew 2:13-23, Luke 2:38-40

After yet another dream featuring another angelic word, Joseph escaped the murderous intentions of Herod by hiding in Egypt till further notice. There they stayed until Herod died. Matthew saw a theological significance in this, as Egypt had been the setting for the great liberation known as the Exodus. The nation as God's son had been called out of Egypt. How appropriate that Messiah, God's son, also emerge from Egypt.

Herod the Great was not a Jew, but an Idumean, who had been appointed king of Judea by the Roman Senate in 40 BC. When he gained control three years later his reign was noted for great building and refurbishing projects – of theatres, amphitheatres, fortresses, monuments, pagan altars, and not least the Jews' temple at Jerusalem. But he was a paranoid, ruthless, conniving and deceitful tyrant. He murdered a wife, three sons, a mother-in-law, a brother-in-law, an uncle and many others. He was not to be crossed. When no report was forthcoming from the magi, it was in a furious yet calculating mood that he gave the order to massacre all the baby boys of Bethlehem. The community grief was immense.

Joseph had two more dreams, the first of which informed him that the coast was clear to return. Herod was dead, but had changed his will so that the worst of his sons, Archelaus, succeeded him instead of Antipas. So a second dream directed Joseph back to Nazareth in Galilee.

The temple visit at the age of twelve
Luke 2:41-52

The one piece of information we have about Jesus' boyhood was a visit to the temple in Jerusalem at Passover time. Joseph and Mary were quite used to this pilgrimage as part of a sizeable group from Nazareth. The men travelled with men and women with women. On the return journey home, it emerged at the end of the day that Jesus was missing, both of his parents assuming that he was with the other group. He in fact was still at the temple, listening to the Jewish teachers, asking questions and giving intelligent answers. Luke didn't say anything as to where Jesus stayed overnight or with whom. Were Zachariah and Elizabeth still alive? Did he and John meet up? We do not know. The point Luke wanted his readers to know was that, in the context of Mary's worried agitation, Jesus was acutely conscious that the temple was *his Father's house.* That was deliberately meant to be an astounding and arresting phrase. Not even David, Solomon or Isaiah would dare to refer to the temple as 'my Father's house.' But the twelve year old Messiah did. And the clear implication is that Jesus expected Joseph and Mary to have realised it too. This wasn't a case of adolescent audacity, or a slip of the tongue. Twenty or so years later, Jesus would be back at that very same venue as a mature man, and would speak in the same vein. His Father's house was a house of prayer.

And so Messiah has arrived. But we are to be warned. This intelligent boy was not going to be the conventional type. His mother discovered this early on, and so too would the Jewish people. Eighteen years would pass without any further comment. But then the full impact of this life would start to be felt.

CHAPTER 3

Meet the Messiah

In central Europe the sources of the rivers Rhine, Rhone, Po and Danube are not so very far from each other. But the Rhine flows to the North Sea, while the Rhone flows southwards to the Mediterranean; the Po and the Danube both flow eastwards, the Po to the Adriatic and the Danube to the Black Sea. I remember this from a Geography lesson in which we were taught the meaning of the geographical term 'watershed'. In the UK it means a distinct divide. And it is in that sense that the word is used in all sorts of contexts – social, political, historical, cultural, religious and scientific. For example, nine o'clock in the evening is supposed to be a TV 'watershed', before which the viewer can assume the programme is fit for family viewing.

Historical 'watersheds' have often been linked with the names of people – like Galileo, da Vinci, Luther, Newton, Einstein, Gandhi, Mandela and many more.

Of particular interest to Christians is the watershed created by the coming of Jesus.

The sudden appearance of Messiah's herald
Matthew 3:1-12, Mark 1:2-8, Luke 3:1-20

A new era

After the episode in the temple when he was twelve, the next mention of Jesus was when he and John both emerged publicly at the age of thirty. This was quite a dramatic event, but more importantly it was also the start of a new era, a strategic step forward in God's plan and time schedule. Until the ministry of John, the message of the Hebrew law and the prophets had been proclaimed, but in its proclamation it remained unfulfilled. With John's arrival, that changed. When the good news of the kingdom of God started to be preached a new day dawned – the day of fulfilment (Luke 16:16, Matthew 11:12,13). Jesus later would tell the Jewish leaders that 'John came to you to show you the way of righteousness' (Matthew 21:32), and although the leadership rejected John's message, many people took on board the truth of the kingdom and entered into it. With the public ministry of John, all prior expectations were about to be realised. This was it – there was no plan B.

Nothing of essence had changed from the angel's announcement before his birth that John was destined to prepare a people ready for the Lord (Luke 1:17). John himself, as the promised herald of the Lord, was conscious that two particular prophetic Scriptures were being fulfilled: 'See, I will send my messenger, who will prepare the way before me' (Malachi 3:1); 'A voice of one calling: "In the desert prepare the way for the Lord; make straight in the wilderness a highway for our God"' (Isaiah 40:3).

This was why John at first appeared in the sparsely populated Judean wilderness near the Dead Sea. But crowds were soon drawn. Coming in the spirit and power of Elijah, he purposely identified with him and even dressed like him – wearing a rough garment with a leather waist belt (2 Kings 1:8). Fashion was unimportant to him. Well acquainted with the prophecy of his parents, he was entirely unashamed of his distinctive prophetic calling, making no apology for his stand. Even Herod Antipas knew he was a holy and a righteous man (Mark 6:20), and was afraid of him. Sustaining himself with a basic diet of dried locusts and mountain honey, which was a good source of mineral and protein, he stayed focused on his mission. God was coming to his people to deliver them spiritually, just as literally as he had restored them geographically from their exile in Babylon.

Thirty years earlier his father had also said how this would unfold. The preparation of the Lord's path entailed bringing to 'his people the knowledge of salvation through the forgiveness of their sins' (Luke 1:77). This meant that John's emphasis as the herald of the Messianic age was new and distinctive. The Jews may continue to insist on thinking in terms of an earthly king and a political kingdom, but as John introduced this king he was careful to announce that the kingdom near at hand was the kingdom of *heaven*. And this would not, as was widely supposed, be a day of deliverance from Israel's foreign oppressors, but a critical day of reckoning for Israel itself. The axe was laid to the root of any spiritual tree not planted by the Father.

The baptism of repentance

If mankind was ever to see God's salvation, there first had to be a moral response so dramatic that it squared with the sort of manual activity which thoroughly transformed the contours of the landscape – valleys filled in, hills levelled, twists and turns straightened out, and a smooth surface prepared.

John was the preacher known as 'the baptizing one.' Using the River Jordan at Bethany (near the Dead Sea) and at Aenon (further north), he preached a baptism that was singularly marked by repentance. His cry went out, 'Repent, for the kingdom of heaven is near' (Matthew 3:2). It's vital to understand what he meant by this. Very clearly, the core of his message concerning the kingdom of God was that forgiveness of sins was contingent on people's radical change of mind that resulted in forsaking their sinful lifestyles. John was advocating realistic thinking and positive action. He demanded a change of moral direction. If they faced up to that issue, confessed their sins and turned away from them, he baptized them as a public sign of God's forgiveness.

It cannot be stressed enough that for John the core issues were those of sins, repentance and forgiveness. This was how people were to prepare for the arrival of this king. It was nothing other than what the coming king expected – a deep and thorough change of attitude.

This aspect of John's preaching was so important that when John was imprisoned and unable to speak publicly, Jesus himself took up the same imperative text, 'Repent, for the kingdom of heaven is near' (Matthew 4:17). If any kingdom is to succeed, an able ruler must have co-operating and submissive subjects. As Moses had discovered, if people were hard of heart, then in the interests of practicality the rules had to be changed (Matthew 19:8,9). But the kingdom of God would insist that it was the people who had to change. Only then would sins be remitted and judgement averted.

John shocked some in his audience by declaring that it simply would not do to sidestep this issue by playing the 'chosen people' card – that they were descended from their father Abraham. God could create children for Abraham out of stones! He knew only too well the truth about those in the Jewish religious establishment, and when he addressed the Pharisees and Sadducees as a 'brood of vipers' his vital point was whether or not a person showed the 'fruits of repentance.' God was looking for the practical and tangible proof that was in keeping with a change of heart. So he called upon all his listeners to personally examine their inner selves.

The results of repentance became clear when the people asked what they should do. John emphasised several essential virtues – of generosity, honesty, gentleness, justice and contentment. Whoever had surplus clothes and food should share with those deprived of life's basics; tax collectors were to collect no more than the set sum and avoid extortion; soldiers were told, 'Don't extort money,' 'Don't accuse people falsely' and 'Be content with your pay.' He even had a word of rebuke for Herod Antipas, which was a move that would spell his demise and death.

A steady stream of people from Jerusalem and the province of Judea kept coming for baptism. But these were not Gentile proselytes who were becoming Jews. These were members of the Jewish people who saw they needed to repent and come back to the true kingdom of God.

Later, Jesus in a dialogue with the Pharisees would establish the point that John's baptism was from heaven and not from men and that their proper response, therefore, should have been to have believed him

(Luke 20:4-8). John had shown them the right way. The chief priests, elders and teachers of the law were well aware that the majority of public opinion considered him a prophet. But they rejected him, while many of the despised groups, such as the prostitutes and tax collectors, applied his words personally and actually got into the kingdom (Matthew 21:32).

John's testimony to Messiah

As well as indicating what Messiah expected of the people, John also outlined what they could expect of their Messiah. The man who was soon to come after him was far greater than he in terms of both ability and worth. John was alluding to the powerful king mentioned in Isaiah 40. According to John Jesus would be a spiritual diagnostician *par excellence* who could precisely, methodically and consistently discern all the issues presented by situations and people. And it was in such a majestic and imposing presence that he felt he was not good enough even to bend down and untie his sandals. In Jewish society, when a guest came into a house the loosing of his sandals was done by a slave. John saw himself as Messiah's slave. This was not a case of false modesty on his part. He had a very good reason and gave it.

He explained that he could only baptize the people with water, but Messiah would baptize his people 'with the Holy Spirit.' John's water baptism was one thing; Jesus' Holy Spirit baptism was something else. John was talking about the fullest possible work of the Holy Spirit – and only Jesus could make it happen. At the very outset, then, this was a clear pointer to the revolutionary idea of a spiritual new birth, which Paul appropriately referred to later as 'the washing of rebirth and renewal by the Holy Spirit' (Titus 3:5). This involved a purification and cleansing that was integral to the promised new covenant. And John said that all of that was beyond his power to achieve. Only Messiah Jesus could give the Holy Spirit.

John's word was reliable. He performed no spectacular or dramatic miracles, because that was not his brief. But everything he said about Jesus was true. His testimony to the Messiah was with a view that men might believe as well as repent (John 1:7). And many did (John 10:41-42).

The later testimony of the New Testament writers reinforced John's word concerning the baptism in the Spirit accomplished by Jesus. It was a baptism of initiation, as the life of God was breathed into believers, thus making them a new creation and conferring on them a new spiritual status. Only through the Holy Spirit could they take their place in God's community, known as the 'body' of Christ; God's intention was that his church throbbed with divine life – and that could only happen when all the members drank from one Spirit (1 Corinthians 12:13).

This invariably involved a new spiritual experience, for only through the Spirit would God take his rightful place in their lives (Acts 1:5, 2:4). In fact, Paul would define this new kingdom as nothing other than an internal reign of righteousness, peace and joy which was invested in the Holy Spirit (Romans 14:17). The kingdom of God was a matter of the heart. This was indeed a watershed.

The Spirit-endowed and morally worthy Messiah

Messiah Jesus is the supreme attraction of the gospel. This cannot be improved on. Any competition is futile and blasphemous.

His baptism
Matthew 3:13-17, Mark 1:9-11, Luke 3:21-22

The gospel writers want to fix our attention on a *humble, unique and Spirit endowed Messiah.* So there came a day when Jesus came from Nazareth to be baptized publicly by John in the Jordan River. John at first strongly protested. He was the one in need of Jesus' Spirit baptism. In his words to Jesus we can detect real surprise to the point of incredulity – 'I need to be baptized by you, and do *you* come to *me*?' (Matthew 3:14, italics mine). We can readily understand John's objection. He knew that Jesus did not need to repent, because he had no sin to repent of, nor was there any area of failure in his life which he needed to address.

But Jesus was insistent. And we are told why. First, he wanted to show that he identified with John and approved of John's message. John after all was his herald. That was why Jesus said that it was appropriate that *together* they fulfilled all righteousness. He used the plural not the singular and saw his baptism as a fulfilment of God's will. He was probably conscious of the same scripture that he would quote shortly before his crucifixion: that as the servant of the Lord he was to be numbered with the transgressors. His baptism was the first deliberate public step of his willingness to associate and identify with people who were sinners, though he would never be guilty of any sin. We should be grateful.

But there was a deeper reason for his baptism – one which was connected to the person he was and his public revelation to the nation. John the Baptist said, '… the reason I came baptizing with water was that he might be revealed to Israel' (John 1:31). His baptism was intended to reveal him as the one who alone could give life. Therefore, when he emerged from the water and the heavens split like a garment, the Spirit of God came upon him and a voice addressed him from heaven, 'You are my Son, whom I love; with you I am well pleased' (Luke 3:22). Jesus was certainly praying at this time, but it was not a prayer of confession. John the Baptist said he saw all of this and added that God had personally told him what would happen and that it was a sign: 'The man on whom you see the Spirit come down and remain is he who will baptize with the Holy Spirit. I have seen and I testify that this is the Son of God' (John 1:33,34). Jesus was declared by the Father to be the Son of God; he was publicly empowered with the Spirit of God. Thus assured of his status, approved by the Father and equipped with the Spirit (Isaiah 11:2) he was marked out for a special mission and remains the object of our faith.

His temptation
Matthew 4:1-11, Mark 1:12-13, Luke 4:1-13

The gospel writers also present a *Messiah who is morally worthy.*

When Jesus was tempted, Satan showed him no favours. He threw everything at him. Jesus was 'tempted in every way, just as we are – yet was without sin' (Hebrews 4:15). The wilderness was lonely, dangerous and could be depressing. It was the haunt of wild beasts like the wolf, the boar, the hyena, the jackal and the leopard. But Jesus' found strength in the Holy Spirit, Scripture meditation and the support of angels.

Matthew and Luke say that at this moment Jesus 'was led' by the Spirit, while Mark used the vivid idea of being 'Spirit driven.' The forty days in the wilderness were under the direct guidance of the Holy Spirit as was the entire earthly life of Jesus from his birth to his death and resurrection. Jesus, meditating on Scripture, was engrossed in the book of Deuteronomy. Angels came to serve and kept it up till he was cheered and strengthened.

The first temptation was verbalised as 'If you are the Son of God, tell these stones to become bread.' What Satan meant was that Jesus as the Son of God should use his miraculous powers on himself and his physical needs. He was hungry, he needed to eat; he was entitled to exercise his rights and use his position to enjoy some privileges. He should indulge himself. What was the harm of it? Satan brought into play all his wiles and craftiness, speaking quite innocently and plausibly as if he actually cared. It was a temptation *to be self-orientated*. Jesus met it with the assertion from Deuteronomy 8:3 that man must depend on God and not on his own abilities. 'Man does not live on bread alone, but on every word that comes from the mouth of God.' Satan was resisted on the grounds that spiritual things are more important than material things. After all, the soul can't be fed on bread. The material can't satisfy the spiritual.

Jesus' scriptural reply advocated a complete dependence upon God. This led Satan to take up the idea of trust in his next temptation. He showed he could quote a verse too. Satan's suggestion was that Jesus threw himself down from the temple, 300 feet down to the Kidron valley. He would survive, for he was special – or so his Father had said at his baptism! He came to Jesus as an angel of light, maintaining that his viewpoint was quite scriptural. Angels, so said the Scripture, would be there to prevent Jesus from coming to any harm. But Jesus knew that the truth did not lie in random texts taken out of context. They may well maximise the element of surprise if used as a mechanical trap. And that was how Satan was using them. Jesus' meditation on scriptural truth was different, however. For in meditation, scripture conditions one's thinking, and controls the mind, so that the spiritual principles behind life on earth come into clear focus. It was such meditation on Scripture which exposed the issues here, for truth lies in the phrase, 'It is *also* written' (Matthew 4:7, italics mine). This was a temptation *to be famous.* But to aim for fame necessarily involved pleasing the notions of men. Jesus dealt with the issue by asserting that God's promises were not meant to encourage presumption. God is not a fascinating novelty or a game to be played for human advantage. He is not someone we can manipulate at will. 'Do not put the Lord your God to the test' came from Deuteronomy 6:16. God was to be obeyed, not experimented with.

The third temptation was *to be powerful.* Jesus could have the whole world in his grip if he lowered his standards just the once in the interests of practicality. If Jesus would acknowledge Satan, listen to his advice and be influenced by him, then what Adam forfeited would be restored. Do as Satan said and he would be king. This was Satan coming as the roaring lion quite unashamedly pointing to the forbidden thing. Jesus could see that the devil was presenting an illusory short cut. It was an attempt to divert the coming of the kingdom of heaven by bribing the king with the kingdoms of this world. Jesus knew that his Father must fill his vision as the source of power. The promises would not be fulfilled on Jesus' independent initiative. He was responsible to the Father for all that he did. The Father was the motivating force in his life. So Jesus met the temptation with the affirmation that God exclusively was the one to be worshipped and served. 'Worship the Lord your God and serve Him only' (Deuteronomy 6:13).

The Spirit and the Scripture controlled Jesus' motives, aspirations and vision. So he refused selfishness, fame and power for the things that really mattered – God's word, God's plan and true worship. The temptation of Jesus showed that God's Spirit-anointed and chosen king was also morally worthy.

Messiah's early impact

Matthew 4:12-22, Mark 1:14-20, Luke 4:14-32

Endowed with the Spirit and morally worthy, Jesus was then presented as *a Messiah who spoke with authority.*

The public ministry of John had been permanently curtailed when he was imprisoned by Herod Antipas, and on hearing that news Jesus returned from Judea in the south of the country to Galilee in the north.

He was familiar with Galilee. It was where his family lived and where he had been brought up. Here he proclaimed God's good news in the power of the Holy Spirit and soon became the talking point of the whole territory. At first he was generally appreciated as he taught in the synagogues.

But the kingdom of God made specific demands. Messiah was presented as nothing less than the Light, the Prophet and the Master. And the call of the kingdom that went out was a call to Jesus as that sort of Messiah. It was a call to repentance and a call to discipleship.

The call to Jesus as the light

Jesus went to live not in Nazareth where he had been raised but in town of Capernaum, by the Sea of Galilee. This was the town of his choice. That this area corresponded with the territory that had been allocated in the past to the tribes of Zebulun and Naphtali was a point of tremendous significance to Matthew. He saw the physical presence of Jesus there as a great spiritual light in a region of darkness and death. Wherever he dwelt, his kingship shone out. Matthew saw the Scriptures being fulfilled. He referred to Isaiah 9:1-2: 'Land of Zebulun and land of Naphtali, the way to the sea, along the Jordan, Galilee of the Gentiles – the people living in darkness have seen a great light; on those living in the land of the shadow of death a light has dawned' (Matthew 4:15,16). People had settled down in the darkness of spiritual death, their eyes having got accustomed to the gloom. But when Jesus arrived his coming was a light suddenly switched. Capernaum was later to be censured quite severely by Jesus. The greater their privilege, the greater would be their responsibility. They were in danger of 'sinning against the light.'

The call to Jesus as the prophet

Luke informs us that one of the reasons for the permanent move to Capernaum was the fact that things had already started to turn sour at Nazareth. In the synagogue one Sabbath Jesus chose to read the passage from Isaiah 61: 'The Spirit of the Lord is on me, because he has anointed me to preach good news to the poor. He has sent me to proclaim freedom for the prisoners and recovery of sight for the blind, to release the oppressed, to proclaim the year of the Lords favour' (Luke 4:18,19). After he sat down, still the focus of attention, he said, 'Today this scripture is fulfilled in your hearing.'

From then on, the townsfolk's first and early impressions which had been favourable began to fade away rapidly. Wasn't he simply the son of Joseph? He was surely aspiring to a status beyond his place. Jesus anticipated further opposition as he perceived that they wanted to see visible evidence that the reports of what was happening in Capernaum were in fact real. It was then that Jesus claimed a prophetic status akin to that of Elijah and Elisha. It was par for the course, it seemed, that prophets were never welcomed in their home town. During a three and a half year drought and famine, Elijah was not sent to anyone in Israel, but to a widow living in Zarephath in the territory of Sidon. And Elisha his successor healed no one in Israel who had leprosy – just Naaman the Syrian. Jesus wanted to make his point clear. While the people of Nazareth refused to acknowledge who he was, he would do no mighty work there.

For those in the synagogue that day, this was a push too far. Overcome with anger they dragged Jesus out of town, and were mad enough to throw him over the cliff. Something happened, however, which hindered them because Jesus calmly walked through the crowd and went away. Nazareth had blown it.

The call to repentance and faith

From that moment Jesus concentrated on proclaiming his message which Mark was careful to describe as 'the good news of God', that is, the good news that came from God. It was to be believed because its source could be no higher. Jesus took the same line as John and proclaimed the arrival of the kingdom of God and the necessity of repentance in order to enter it.

'The time has come!' The years of promise had finally given way to the period of fulfilment. The apostle Paul would later tell the churches in Galatia that the new era of redemption and adoption into God's family began right on schedule. For 'when the time had fully come, God sent his Son, born of a woman, born under the law, to redeem those under the law, that we might receive the full rights of sons' (Galatians 4:4,5).

'The kingdom of God is near. Repent and believe the good news!' Here was a universal and general call. The kingdom demanded a change of mind which involved confession of sin and a turning away from sins. This crisis called for faith in the message of Jesus that the kingdom of God had arrived with the presence of the King.

The call to personal discipleship
Matthew 4:18-22, Mark 1:16-20, Luke 5:1-11

Andrew, Simon Peter, James and John were the first four of the group we know as the twelve apostles. Jesus was already acquainted with these fishermen he was about to call, and Jesus was not a total stranger to them either.

We know that Andrew had already taken time out of his work as a fisherman on the Sea of Galilee to travel down to Judea with others from Galilee in order to imbibe the teachings of John the Baptist. At Bethany on the Jordan he had heard John speak of a person he had baptized who was the Son of God and the Lamb of God, and Andrew had been present when John identified that special person as Jesus (John 1:35-42). With a friend (possibly John the apostle) Andrew had spent some quality time with Jesus, and the very next day had returned to introduce his own brother Simon to Jesus, convinced in his own mind that they had found the Messiah. The group had subsequently returned to Galilee and resumed their fishing which was what they were doing when Jesus turned up again.

But their fisherman partners, John and James, also knew Jesus. They were probably his first cousins. Their mother, Salome was to become a reliable supporter of Jesus, present at his last moments. All four gospel writers mention her alongside three other women, all of whom curiously were named Mary – Mary the mother of Jesus, Mary Magdalene and another Mary who was the wife of Clopas and the mother of James and Joseph (compare Matthew 27:55-56 with Mark 15:40-41 and John 19:25). Of these four women John mentioned the last two Marys by name, but referred to the other two women as 'the mother of Jesus' and 'his mother's sister'. It has therefore been reasonably deduced that Mary and Salome were sisters, that James and John were the cousins of Jesus, and therefore were also related to the family of John the Baptist. This would explain quite a lot, not least that when Jesus was dying it was the most natural thing for him to ask John to look after his mother – who would have been John's aunt.

The accounts in Matthew and Mark of the call of these four fishermen to discipleship are almost identical. Luke's account is longer and has a different emphasis. He shines his spotlight on Simon Peter and does not mention Andrew. Also Luke places the incident after the first tour of Galilee (Luke 4:42-44) whereas Matthew and Mark place it at the very outset.

The evidence suggests, however, that it is the same incident, with Mark and Matthew giving us the bare bones. James and John figure in each of the accounts – they were getting their nets ready for the next haul of fish. With their father Zebedee they ran an extensive business in partnership with Andrew and Simon (Luke 5:7,10). All the accounts conclude with the fishermen becoming permanent followers of Jesus, leaving boat, family, hired servants and the business; and they all make the same point – the assurance that in the future they would catch men for the kingdom. If Luke's account was referring to another event, it would mean that the fishermen had gone back on their earlier commitment as recorded by Mark and Matthew.

The point being made was that Jesus' authority was real and had a worthy end result. At his call, men would make their decision to leave their jobs, family, employees and business in order to become something that he promised to make them. It would admittedly be a long process, involving many slip ups, and even serious low points, because discipleship was an ongoing relationship where they were the learners and Jesus was the teacher. But Jesus could do it, would do it – and finally did do it. He made fishers of men out of fishermen.

There is a very good reason why Luke placed the story where he did in his gospel. He had just described how the Nazareth crowd had relegated Jesus to the mere status of being Joseph's son. But Luke wanted to show how Jesus had hidden qualities, innate proficiency and relevant know-how that needed to be revealed. He was far much more than what appeared on the surface. This carpenter knew how to catch fish! Jesus, pressed by the crowd, taught from the relative comfort of Peter's boat. Peter's boat became his pulpit – just as later Peter's fishing net would be replaced by the gospel net. Then Peter and his crew listened to Jesus' words as he spoke to the crowd. We do not know what Jesus said. But when he had finished Jesus gave the master fisherman a precise instruction as to how to go about his job. Peter was a tired and weary man who had just completed a rather fruitless night shift. At first he protested but with a resigned shrug of the shoulders he reluctantly complied. The words, 'If you say so,' were not spoken at all enthusiastically. But at least Peter did as he was told. The result was truly beyond belief. James and John were also dumbfounded, as they witnessed nets that were in danger of tearing and boats in danger of sinking. Peter's self-confidence and pride were replaced by his humble confession. He was in no doubt that he had witnessed a miracle. He saw himself as a sinful man.

Now it was in that context that Jesus said to Peter, 'Don't be afraid; from now on you will catch men' (Luke 5:10). He would take them alive for the kingdom. And it was then and there that the four of them left their business for active service of Christ. We can now understand why.

Peter would indeed be a catcher of men. On the Day of Pentecost, in the context that the crucified and risen Jesus was Lord and Messiah, he preached the message of the kingdom that John and Jesus had done – that people should turn from their sins, be baptized and receive forgiveness. Three thousand people were added to the group that day (Acts 2:36-41). After the healing of the lame man in the name of Jesus and by the power of his resurrection life, Peter again proclaimed that the listeners should repent and turn to God for the forgiveness of their sins. Many more believed, the number reaching five thousand (Acts 3:19–4:4). Every day in the temple and in people's homes as the good news about Messiah Jesus was proclaimed the number of disciples kept growing (Acts 4:42–6:1).

In this way Jesus' prophecy was to come true. In Matthew 13:47-50, Jesus would liken the kingdom of heaven to a net let down into the lake to catch all kinds of fish. This gospel net was to be immersed into the sea of humanity with no discrimination. Some fish would escape the net and all of the attempts of the fishermen to catch them. But the net would be filled, and when it was it would be landed and the contents inspected and scrutinised. This was the fishing for men that Jesus was concerned with.

But we are running ahead of ourselves. All of this later success issued from the impact Jesus made on men and women as the light of the world and God's reliable prophet. He was announced as the Son of God who was endued with the Spirit of God. He was the Master who was resolute against temptation and a leader of men. This is but the start of the gospel portrait of the Messiah. And in the next chapter we will see that he impressed the people just as much in what he said as in what he did.

CHAPTER 4

Authority in Deed and Word

Travelling throughout Galilee

The Summary: Matthew 4:23-25

Matthew summarised the remarkable ministry that was about to take place in Galilee. The good news about the Kingdom was proclaimed in local synagogues and was accompanied by a successful and completely unrestricted healing ministry. Nothing it seemed was beyond Jesus' ability, and the news of this rabbi/healer soon spread far and wide, even throughout Syro-Phoenicia to the whole of Syria.

He attracted those who were suffering in any and every way. Some were conscious of physical problems or psychological disorders that were not related to anything else. Others had conditions with more complicated causes such as birth injuries, social infection, a careless personal lifestyle or demon possession. Jesus could tell. His ministry was not a 'one size fits all' approach. He dealt with folk individually. Sometimes he would converse with the person, sometimes he would say nothing and on one occasion he even addressed the fever from which a woman was suffering just as he would speak to waves and wind and more often demons. Thus it was a common sight to see large crowds following him that came from Galilee, the Decapolis region (the ten towns east of Jordan), Jerusalem, Judea, and the southern land on the other side of the Jordan. Of course, there would have been sceptics. But this was no ordinary person and he was on no ordinary mission.

We know from Luke's record, that Jesus made three separate tours of the region of Galilee (Luke 4:42-44, 8:1-3, 9:1-6). Matthew made no such distinction but treated the Galilean ministry as just one bloc and arranged his material to suit a thematic or topical approach. He wished to show the *authority of Jesus in word and deed* as he promoted the kingdom. Thus, the verbal authority that we will see was so evident in the Sermon on the Mount (Matthew 5–7) would in the interests of his theme be carried over into the visual and practical authority of his selection of miracles in chapters 8 and 9 of his gospel.

Take just one example. Matthew set the healing of the centurion's servant side by side with the calming of the storm (Matthew 8:5-13, 18-27). In fact they took place at two different times. We know this when we use as reference points the same events recorded by all three writers. Luke placed the healing of the centurion's servant (Luke 7:1-10) a whole chapter *after* his record of the Sabbath controversies involving the healing of the man with the withered hand, while Matthew inserted his account four chapters *before* those same events. In Mark the calming of the storm (Mark 4:35-41) comes after the visit of Jesus' family and the parable of the sower, which Luke (Luke 8:22-25) said belonged to the second Galilean tour. But Matthew inserted his record five chapters earlier next to the healing of the centurion's servant. Why?

It all becomes clear when we realise the specific point Matthew was making. If Jesus really had the sort of authority he claimed and demonstrated, then the proper response on the part of his audience would be to trust him and do what he said. Now that is precisely what the Roman centurion did when he talked maturely about the notion of authority. He knew he was not worthy that Jesus came to his house. A word from him would be enough. Any instructions the centurion gave officially to his subordinates carried the imperial authority under which he functioned, and Jesus, he recognised, also operated under a delegated authority. Jesus was well impressed. He commended the centurion's response as one of 'great faith', enhanced by the fact that this man was not a Jew but a Roman. And yet, in the same eighth chapter, Matthew highlighted an instance of what Jesus termed 'little faith', which was not displayed by foreigners or rank unbelievers but by disciples who were near to him. The contrast was obvious, but Matthew drew it deliberately. If Jesus had authority over things which were as diverse as distant out-of-sight situations and the immediate peril of the forces of nature, then he should be trusted.

The Manifesto of the Kingdom: the Sermon on the Mount
Matthew 5–7; see also Luke 6:17-49

General elections are usually preceded by the publication of the various manifestos of the political parties. The idea is that the voters will know what to expect if the party they voted for gets into power. It's a good idea, but it cannot be guaranteed to work.

Jesus' discourse was a statement of what the kingdom of heaven was all about. He was not campaigning for office, however, nor was he looking for votes. But the disciples who had committed to it and those yet to enter it needed to know its character, standards and implications. So this sermon was Jesus' own exposition of the nature of the kingdom. For those who had faced up to their lives, repented of their sin and begun to follow him, this realm they had entered enshrined the righteous rule of God, and was equated with the concept of the spiritual family of God. It was in this connection that Jesus presented God as the Father of his disciples, and himself as their focal point. The Father was the head of the family and Jesus was the one who spoke with authority in that family.

This foundational concept kept surfacing. It was God their heavenly Father who was to be praised through his followers' good works (5:16); when they showed love towards even their enemies and prayed for their persecutors they displayed precisely the character of their heavenly Father (5:44,45) who was their mentor, their goal and their example (5:48). It was as their Father that God gave them gracious rewards (6:1,4,6,18); it was their Father who knew their needs and to whom they were to pray (6:8,9,32); it was their heavenly Father who both forgave them and insisted unequivocally that they too forgive (6:14,15);

everything they did, even down to the practice of fasting, was to be done before their Father's all seeing gaze (6:17,18); it was their heavenly Father who provided food for the birds (6:26) and would give good things to his spiritual children when they asked (7:11). Right throughout the sermon, the person to whom the disciples were accountable was their heavenly Father.

The Father was also, in a different sense, Jesus' own Father. Jesus said, 'Not everyone who says to me, Lord, Lord, will enter the kingdom of heaven, but only he who does the will of my Father who is in heaven' (Matthew 7:21). The followers of Messiah Jesus were to recognise their accountability to his Father and submit to his authority and rule.

Jesus proceeded to talk about three truths that related first to *the citizens* of the kingdom, then to its *ethos* or atmosphere and finally how it may be entered.

It would be revolutionary and refreshing stuff!

The citizens of the kingdom
Matthew 5:1-16

The community of Jesus' disciples, then, could be viewed as citizens of the kingdom, the king's subjects and the children of the Father. Two main things are said about them.

They have received a special blessing
Matthew 5:1-9

We refer to these statements as the Beatitudes, opening as they do with the announcement of blessing, but they are better seen as exclamations that paint a picture of Christian disciples as privileged people because of God's kindness and grace.

'O the happiness of...' would be a more accurate translation. The same word describes those whose transgressions are forgiven (Romans 4:7), those who have died belonging to the Lord (Revelation 14:13) and those who were invited to the wedding supper of the Lamb (Revelation 19:9). They are all happy. In fact Paul applied the adjective to God (1 Timothy 1:11) which is not at all strange when we realise that the word literally means 'not subject to fate.' Because God is not subject to fate or fortune, all joys rest in Him. And when Jesus described his followers as 'happy', he meant that they were not under the influence of luck or chance. The spin-off would be anything from relieved contentment and pleasurable delight to expressions of the most joyful elation.

The first part of each statement is a description of the sort of person who was probably present that day. They were so different from one another. Some were in obvious need while others displayed eager zeal. There is no need to look for a causal link between the first part and the last part of each statement. The second part is the cause of the happiness in each particular case, simply reflecting the change that took place in the person because of his or her response to the call of the kingdom. It emphasises a particular aspect of blessing.

All sorts of folk were listening. There were those who had no influence or prestige but just a spiritual need; but they had responded to Jesus, and had their stake in the kingdom. The lives of others were even at that moment full of sorrow and grief; they needed to know that in the kingdom real spiritual comfort was to be found. Some were there who found it hard to stand up for their rights in the face of injustice; but they would not lose out in the kingdom of God where it was the meek who were the heirs. And then there were those who were passionate about goodness and holiness; well, they had come to the right person; for them the kingdom would satisfy all their aspirations. People had turned up who were known for their lives of mercy, care and concern to their fellow human beings; in the kingdom of God they as recipients would be able to appreciate his gift of mercy to them. Some in the audience had already realised the importance of an inner life that was honest, transparent and free from hypocrisy; in the kingdom they could expect to encounter God. And those who were already putting a premium on peace making would find that they would be quite at home in the family of God.

Thus the truly happy person was not the self-confident, self-satisfied, self-possessed, self-assertive, self-sufficient, self-made, self-conscious person, but anyone who followed Messiah and became through the grace of God a changed character. This was such encouraging stuff!

It came with a warning, however. The kingdom community would evoke a curious reaction in society (5:10-12) because of its association with Messiah and righteousness. Persecution would come and should be expected. It may take form of political pressure, social insult or legal slander. But when it came, Messiah's people were to focus on their heavenly reward and their spiritual pedigree.

They perform a unique function
Matthew 5:13-16

Jesus taught that his disciples should not be distracted by opposition. Just like God's prophets of old, they were vital to society. They were 'the salt of the earth' and 'the light of the world.' Jesus was underlining the crucial difference between the members of his kingdom and the surrounding world in which they were set. Everyone was familiar with salt; it was transported everywhere either from the Mediterranean Sea or from the salt marshes by the Dead Sea. Its common use was as a disinfectant and a fertiliser. Whereas we have flush toilets, then they used shovels of salt. In a spiritually infectious society his disciples made a difference just by being what they were where they were.

Jesus used two analogies concerning light. The light of a city on a hill could not be hidden because the white limestone of the buildings would glare in the sun. Inside Jewish homes, a lamp would be seen on a projecting stone in the wall. The whole point of lamps was that they were placed on the stand, and not under the earthenware bowl that measured out grain. Because society needed spiritual, moral and social light, the followers of Christ were not to hide their good deeds even in an evil world of persecution. They were to shine to the glory and praise of their Father in heaven. The light in this instance was not talk, but good deeds. Messiah's disciples were to walk the walk.

The atmosphere or ethos of the kingdom

This kingdom was one of real righteousness. In fact the two ideas – of righteousness and the kingdom – come together more than once: the kingdom belonged to those who were persecuted for the sake of righteousness (5:10); and all were exhorted in their search to make God's kingdom and his righteousness their top priority (6:33).

There was a superior righteousness to be found in Messiah Matthew 5:17–20

As Jesus affirmed the purpose of his mission, he had to speak somewhat negatively in order to correct any wrong conclusions. We must get to grips with what he was saying here, for he was making a vital point in a specific given context. His rather bold assertion was that he had come as the fulfilment of the Old Testament Scriptures. But he knew that his ministry would be misrepresented in some hard line Jewish religious quarters especially when things like food laws were bound to change along with other sacrificial and ceremonial regulations. But no one should interpret his ministry as a subversive process of abolition. What was happening before their eyes was the achievement of the ultimate goal, the full and final completion of God's purposes so that nothing was missing. Folk would be guilty of a great misrepresentation therefore if all they saw was abolition.

Jesus had the highest possible view of the Old Testament Scriptures and upheld their authority. He said that everything was to stay in place until all was fulfilled. True righteousness resided in Messiah himself as the dominating focal point of the Scriptures, but folk had lost sight of this core message. And Jesus as their Messiah was standing before them, repeating the claim he had made in the Nazareth synagogue. From now on he was to be the reference point.

He did not promise that the Old Testament was to remain fixed in concrete, never to be changed. What he did say was that, in his person, what was happening to the law and the prophets was not destruction but fulfilment.

A man bought an old cottage in the countryside. In addition to spacious land, a good view, four walls and a roof, there was not much else. His purpose was to make the place habitable. So he lived on site in a caravan and built new walls around the old building, and ultimately when the enlarged house was completed, he took down the old shell that had been enclosed. The project involved structural change. But he had not acquired the property to keep it as it was, or to destroy it, but to live in it as was its purpose. His activities were those of transformation not abolition.

Years ago, the A5 arterial road that links London with the ferry port at Holyhead and Ireland was in some places hopelessly inadequate to cope with the increasing volume of traffic. The contractors moved in and proceeded to dig up the single carriageway which involved the inevitable disruption to the movement of traffic. It may have seemed that they were destroying the road, but the truth was far different. The aim was to improve it, to make it efficient. Today the A5 around Shrewsbury is unrecognisable from what it once was. Many of the older landmarks have disappeared, but it is evident that the workmen had come to preserve the A5 as a major link in the road system.

Likewise, Jesus was showing the direction in which the Old Testament had always pointed. He was its authoritative interpreter. In themselves they were incomplete. But a new era was inaugurated when he came. The Old Testament Scriptures prophesied until John the Baptist, but from then on it was the era of the forceful advance of the kingdom of heaven as the good news was proclaimed (Matthew 11:11-15; Luke 16:16-17). Paul would later make the same point. Only Messiah could give life. The purpose of the law was to point us to him so that we might be justified by faith (Galatians 3:19-25).

The internal root of righteousness
Matthew 5:21–48

So it was that Jesus spoke in a very arresting way. Five times he said 'You have heard it was said … but I tell you …' He was interested in the hearts of men. The law had always been about loving the Lord with heart, soul and strength, and neighbours too (Deuteronomy 6:4,5). It was such a shame that over time this ideal had been reduced to a tiny scroll with no more significance than that of a charm. The inner life was crucial. Man's mouth expressed only what was in his heart (Matthew 12:33-35). An unclean heart that bred evil thoughts made a man unclean (Matthew 15:18-20). And the Lord, never swayed by external appearances, always looks at the heart (1 Samuel 16:7). This was why Jesus, as the final authority, turned his attention to the privacy of a man's soul. If things were put right at the source, the fountain would be clear. And it was a new heart that the prophets had promised in the new covenant (Ezekiel 33).

This was why Jesus therefore identified the seeds of murder as hate, anger and contempt (5:21-26). Better to deal with them now in the heart in a spirit of reconciliation and kindness, before it got to any public court and before the day of judgement.

Similarly, the seeds of adultery were lust and selfishness in the heart (5:27-32) which were sustained through what the eyes fixed on. This is the peril of pornography and sexually explicit drama which treats sex as merely a recreational leisure activity. There is no self-restraint in the lustful man and no consideration for others. He must have what he sees. Jesus argued for the sort of self-mastery that ruthlessly would metaphorically pluck out the offending eye and cut off the wayward hand. If a husband in anger or by a whim divorced his wife on any other ground than her unfaithfulness, he would be accountable for any ramifications.

And then there was the whole issue of honesty (5:33-37). He had no time for the masters of hair splitting who declared which oaths were legitimate. People should get a reputation for telling it as it was. Yes meant yes, and No meant no; any additional embellishments came from the evil one.

Similarly a spirit of revenge was to be shunned in favour of one of courage and generosity (5:38-42). The law had checked the wild response of unrestrained vengeance by fixing an exact level of compensation for an injury. This had become the maxim, 'An eye for an eye, and a tooth for tooth.' But when promoting the kingdom in the face of nasty opposition, Jesus' followers were to respond by staying focussed on the mission and not getting distracted by issues of retaliation or self-preservation.

It all could be boiled down to love (5:43-48). The law encouraged loving your neighbour as yourself. Some rabbis extrapolated that your enemy was not your neighbour. So it was allowable to hate him, especially the mixed race of Samaritans who lived between Judea and Galilee. No, said Jesus. Love and prayer even for your enemies was what the Father wanted. When he causes the sun to shine and the rain to fall, it is indiscriminate goodness to the evil as well as the good. God shows love because he is love, not because he wants to get a reward. Pagans and tax collectors were not to be the model for his followers; their Father was the standard.

The growing stem of righteousness
Matthew 6:1-18

The disciples needed to know that true heart righteousness would grow in secret in the two areas of social awareness and God awareness. Jesus used the word 'when' not 'if', meaning he was treating these two areas as an assumption: 'when you give', 'when you pray.' Giving and praying were to be regular features, not occasional optional extras.

Righteousness was a 'hands on' practical thing that took notice of people (6:1-4). Giving towards those in need was, for his followers, to be the expression of a joyful spirit of generosity. So Jesus instilled into his followers the priority of pleasing God and not trying to impress men. Philanthropic service, however, was to remain discreet so that no one knew (6:2-4). It was not a performance to be praised by amazed spectators. It was a quiet fulfilment of God's purpose for his people (Ephesians 2:10) and was both the result and proof of faith (James 2:17,18,20,26). Modest and anonymous generosity is good. It lessens the temptation of pride and does not create unhealthy competition or a sense of indebtedness. This has the Father's approval.

Talking to God was also essential if righteousness was to grow. But this too had to be in secret so that no one knew (6:5-13) because true prayer to God was incompatible with publicity. It never lapsed into clichés. When talking to God, his child was coming to a Father who already knew the situation. What was of first importance was one's attitude, particularly a forgiving spirit that let go of all hurts, grudges and injuries. And when engaged in real prayer, it could well lead to a time of fasting, which again was not meant to be broadcast.

Genuine prayer gave God his rightful place – first place. He was the Father in heaven whose Name was to be hallowed. Prayer therefore was not to be self-centred or self-seeking. The disciples were not to approach God to get what they wanted but to ask that God's will be done on earth. Prayer was primarily a concern for the glory of God and the expansion of his kingdom. It was not a shopping list of items to be ticked off once they were mentioned. There were requests, yes; that God would supply all their necessities, forgive their sins, and lead them so that they overcome evil. But first they were to be concerned about God's name, God's kingdom, and God's will. It still applies.

Jesus gave his disciples a pattern (6:9-13) which was never intended to become a mantra preserved in seventeenth century English.

First there had to be *worshipful approach*. 'Our Father in heaven, Hallowed be your Name'. Together, as brothers and sisters, Messiah's people come to the Father, one who is good to all (5:45), who is perfect (5:48), who loves to reward them (6:4), who knows their need (6:8), who forgives (6:15) and cares (6:26), and gives good things (7:11). He is in heaven (which is his throne), and they are on earth (which is his footstool) – quite close therefore, certainly within spiritual earshot (Isaiah 66:1). They reverently venerate his holy name, protect his reputation and value his self-revelation.

This was to be accompanied by *spiritual alignment*. 'Your kingdom come. Your will be done on earth as it is in heaven'. The priority for Messiah's people was the coming of the kingdom, both as a future global event and as a present personal experience. They wished to see his divine rule and sovereignty increase inexorably till it reached its rightful place, so that the powers of darkness, sin and rebellion were forced to retreat. Paul would describe this as the kingdom of 'righteousness, peace and joy in the Holy Spirit' (Romans 14:17). Allied with the kingdom was submission to God's will, known or unknown, which was accepted in advance by people who bowed before his wisdom. Their tone was to be one of spontaneous co-operation, and glad agreement with an instant, enthusiastic and full obedience so characteristic of heaven.

It was in this context that Jesus encouraged an attitude of *constant dependence* and *receptive trust*. Instead of a frantic anxious storing for the distant future, a day by day trust was encouraged in the faithfulness of God, and a readiness to depend upon him for all that was necessary for life. That trust extended from the supply of daily food to the need for forgiveness. Sins were debts that could not be ignored. They had to be paid or forgiven. Those who were living out forgiveness of others could confidently trust God for his forgiveness of them. But dependence and trust in God also applied to trials and temptations. The Father was to be trusted with leadership. And when any test or ordeal came, his people were to trust his protection from power of the enemy. After all, his kingdom was a powerful, glorious and everlasting one.

The spiritual and social fruit of righteousness Matthew 6:19–7:12

This sort of attitude that pervaded such social awareness and prayer was meant to have specific spiritual consequences, personally and socially. Life was to be lived in the context of relationships.

The personal aspect of this heavenly 'fruit' was described by Jesus as a combination of heavenly treasure, exclusive loyalty and contented trust. These are worth the look.

When Jesus spoke about *storing treasure in heaven* (6:19-23), he was encouraging a purposeful investment in eternity – heaven for the Christian being the realm where there is no decay or loss. That made far better sense than the alternative of earth's uncertainties, which today would be expressed in devaluation and escalating insurance costs. Jesus did not classify worldly wealth as 'true riches' (Luke 16:11). An example of a sound spiritual value judgement was when Moses regarded disgrace for the sake of Messiah as of greater value than the treasures of Egypt, because he was looking ahead to his reward (Hebrews 11:24-26). Jesus presented this sort of investment as a choice that issued in the twin blessings of *heart satisfaction* and *personal enlightenment.* Where their treasure was, their heart would also be. If their eyes were on the kingdom of heaven, their whole body would be full of light. The eye was in fact 'the lamp of the body.'

Jesus followed this with the reminder that *no one could serve two masters* (24). The choice was stark – devotion to one as master meant repudiation of the other. The kingdom didn't tolerate duplicity or divided loyalties on this matter. The two 'masters' in this case were God and Money. Like water and fire, money is a good servant but a bad master. Living to make money is not a valid Christian goal. Materialism and consumerism distract people. They can so easily replace God. God may entrust certain folk with material bounty – but that is stewardship, not ownership. No follower of Christ owns anything. God is the owner. Jesus did not advocate a prosperity gospel. The issue therefore is one of good or bad stewardship of what God entrusts us with.

With those two priorities stated, Jesus exhorted *freedom from all anxiety* (6:25-34). Nothing has changed much with the passage of time. Folk still worry over duties, crises and the unknown future. 'Don't,' said Jesus. The Father feeds the birds and clothes the lilies. The birds have to go and get it, yes; but when they find it they don't store it. And he exhorted his people not to be slaves to fashion either. In his estimation, King Solomon couldn't begin to compete with the adornment God gives continually to the flowers. So they were to trust the Father to provide for them. He knew their need. He didn't want them to get like the pagans. Anyway, worry about life was futile and counterproductive, but trust in God was always fruitful. Yes, Peter would later exhort that we can cast all our anxiety on Him, because He cares for us (1 Peter 5:7), but we can do something more than that. Jesus taught that anxiety was nullified when we sort out our priorities. 'Seek first his kingdom and his righteousness, and all these things will be given to you as well. Therefore do not worry about tomorrow' (6:33,34).

This was such perceptive, relevant and practical stuff. But he was not finished just yet. It needed to be applied to the realm of relationships.

Jesus' followers were to avoid the curse of prejudicial, censorious criticism. To come to a considered opinion based on evaluation and assessment was one thing – and was necessary. But the subjective apportioning of blame, denunciation and condemnation was quite another. His followers were to be known as those who corrected their own faults first in order to help their brothers (7:1-5). If a speck of sawdust or some other foreign matter was obviously irritating their brother's eyes and affecting his vision, the situation called for clear purposeful vision on their part rather than a passive complacent judgemental gaze. The metaphorical plank in their eye wouldn't be at all helpful.

They were to be discerning (7:6) as to human nature. If dogs and pigs don't get what their nature dictates, they will angrily turn on those who offer something else, even if it is valuable and sacred. The spiritual things of God are never playthings indiscriminately to be thrown around, and certainly not to be presented to profane mockers who want to enjoy their sin. That is not being judgmental, but discerning.

It was vital to their discipleship that they kept receiving the good things that God wanted to give (7:7-11); 'asking' meant respectfully stating their dependence upon God; 'seeking' revealed a genuine and diligent interest in spiritual values; 'knocking on the door' indicated a specific and persistent concern about an issue. God would respond, providing all that was needed, in accordance with his status as Father. He would never mock, short-change or opt for the cheap substitute. He would even keep on giving the Holy Spirit to those who kept on asking (Luke 11:13).

And then Jesus summed up the Law with this golden rule: treat others as you want them to treat you (7:12). Put yourself in the other person's shoes – whether it was loneliness, illness, poverty or failure – and having empathised, take action.

It was powerful stuff! Jesus was getting back to the real issue of 'goodness' as defined by the prophet Micah – to do justice, to love mercy and to walk humbly with God (Micah 6:8).

Entry to the kingdom
Matthew 7:13-27

All that was left now was to show the people how they could be part of this kingdom. There were three exhortations

Choose the small gate
Matthew 7:13-14

What seemed to be the obvious and welcoming spacious route, reinforced by its apparent popularity, was in fact an illusion. The broad road led to destruction. It was the narrow path that led to life, though the start of it didn't appear at all promising. Folk should take time and find it. Some did. Jesus would specify later, in different imagery, that he as the shepherd was the gate to salvation and abundant life (John 10:7-10). Jesus with his superior righteousness was the narrow gate. And all who entered the kingdom through him immediately identified with the minority.

Shun the false prophet
Matthew 7:15-23

False prophets had always been around. Outwardly they looked acceptable, often even professing a commission from God. But they are never what they seem. They use camouflage to conceal a ferocious and destructive nature, which especially targets the sort of true spirituality Jesus outlined in this sermon. Wolves in sheep's clothing are only interested in feeding themselves. And they would only increase in number (Matthew 24:11,24).

Messiah's people were to be on the alert, to watch out for them and avoid them. There was nothing good about such deception. As to their source, they spoke the product of their own minds, or borrowed from some other source. As to their message, they talked about the things people wanted to hear – whether it was peace, prosperity, health and well-being. As to their emphasis, they never took God's justice seriously and so never exposed sin. Even to those who had no time for God and despised him the false prophets would say, 'The Lord says: You will have peace. No harm will come to you' (Jeremiah 23:16-18). As to their authority, they used God's name but never listened quietly to God. God never sent them, appointed them or even spoke to them. As to their motive, it was usually something to do with money, power or sexual exploitation.

They could be recognised objectively just as the nature of a tree can be assessed by its fruit. If what the man had prophesied did not come true, he was not to be given a second chance (Deuteronomy 18:20-22). Jesus said that the fact that they may even address him as 'Lord' and claim to have done spiritual service – such as prophecy, teaching, exorcism, miracles – meant nothing. They did not do the will of the heavenly Father. Jesus never knew them, was never acquainted with them, was never introduced to them, and never approved of them. Success as the world assessed it was not a guide as to whether he was one of Messiah's people.

That was sobering stuff! It was meant to be. The key to it all was to put Jesus' words into practice.

Apply the truth
Matthew 7:24-27

He said that those who heard his words and applied them in their lives were wise. To be just a good listener was not enough – in fact it was folly. Jesus would leave his listeners with a vivid picture. Two men, equal in privilege and capability, were engaged in the same project of constructing a place of security for themselves. Their progress was visible and they both finished their projects. Both had the same resources and would encounter the same test. Wind, rain and floods would be unforgiving and show no mercy.

Because one was wise, he built on a rock; he planned ahead and realised that conditions would not always be amenable and calm. Foundations, like the ship's anchor or the roots of a plant, were vital though hidden out of sight. And Jesus attached the greatest importance to what men do not see, but which must be there. The wise man dug deep (Luke 6:48) until he hit the rock, getting rid of the unstable stuff that was never going to be strong enough to support the structure. It was time well spent.

The point being made by the parable concerned the serious shortfall between listening and obeying. Jesus' instructions were meant to be followed in addition to being heard and understood, especially his call to repent; the call he issued was meant to be answered, especially the invitation to come to him and follow him; his teachings were meant to be heeded, especially those concerning the inner life, prayer, forgiveness, investment in eternal values (justice, mercy and fellowship with God), and loyalty to God not money.

The foundation in question was submission to his authority in obedience.

The second man listened and maybe assessed the words; but he did no preparatory work. His house did not survive the test, but fell in ruins. It was a parable issuing the warning that failure to apply Messiah's word would mean that one day temptation would prove too strong, the thought of discipleship too restrictive, loyalty to God too costly and persecution too damaging. Jesus would meet such people in real life.

At the close of this teaching of his, the crowd was amazed. He was not at all like the teachers of the Law. This was authentic; this was indeed authoritative stuff!

But what would they do about it?

CHAPTER 5

Promoting the Kingdom in Galilee

Matthew 8:1–13:58, Mark 1:21–6:6, Luke 4:31–8:56

Matthew telescoped the three phases of the Galilean ministry into one. As a result his is not the chronological order. Also, he does not include some of Luke's material. For those reasons we will try to keep Matthew's theme uppermost in our minds, but look at the ministry in Galilee using Mark and Luke as our guides. We will then get a sense of the momentum of events as they happened.

A major aspect of the good news of the kingdom was the authority that was invested in Messiah. Authority can be both imitated by those who don't have it and abused by those who do; but not with Jesus. He was not a tyrant. The Greek word for 'authority' (*exousia*) means 'out of the original essence' – a word which we may justifiably render in our idiom as 'the genuine article', 'the real thing' or 'the heart of the matter' and therefore 'right'. Jesus as the Son of God was anointed by the Spirit and therefore endowed with authentic wisdom. And it showed.

His authority always had a worthy and purposeful end result – as seen in the call of the disciples; it was open and transparent and could be assessed intellectually – as seen in his teaching in the synagogue; it was exercised supremely for the benefit and deliverance of others – as seen in the casting out of demons; it was infused with kindness – as seen in his healing of diseases; and it was self-authenticating, and therefore magnetic – as seen in the crowds that voluntarily came to listen.

In the Galilean ministry, we can pick out four themes: first we have presented to us the *power and authority of the kingdom*; alongside this Jesus also had to deal with at least four different *negative undercurrents*; the situation therefore called for *clear teaching about the kingdom* which was accompanied by a conclusive *authentication of the king.*

We'll consider these four themes in sequence.

The power and authority of the kingdom
Matthew 8:1–9:17, Mark 1:21–2:22, Luke 4:31–5:39

In the first of his Galilean tours, we are brought face to face with the miraculous. The reporting of unusual events can often be linked with dubious motives. But in Jesus' case there was no hint of any element of entertainment by creating mystery, nor was he engaged in marketing some business project. Money, fame and popularity were not issues. His miracles served to emphasise the truth of deliverance by the power of his *authoritative word* coupled with his *compassionate touch.* He loved people.

Teaching with authority and casting out demons
Mark 1:21-28, Luke 4:31-37

The synagogue in Capernaum afforded a natural opening for Jesus to teach. Capernaum, on the northern shore of the Sea of Galilee, became his home town after he was pointedly rejected in Nazareth (Luke 4:16-31, Matthew 4:13-16). The synagogue service each Sabbath day would have included prayer, praise, a scripture reading and an exposition by a rabbi. Jesus' impact was truly amazing. The people noticed at once the transparency of someone who had no obscure agenda and who did not conform to the practice of expounding tradition. It was obvious that he stood apart from the familiar run-of-the-mill system. His fresh and original teaching was as different from the dull and stiff rabbinical rules as chalk is from cheese. He spoke directly from God. It certainly wowed the people then, although it would soon be rated as heresy by the rabbis.

His was an authority that showed control over the realm of evil spirits, and was exercised for the spiritual benefit of others. A man was present who was in the power of a demon and whose voice spoke for the demon and himself. The demon acknowledged that it had nothing in common with Jesus. Demons recognised him as 'The Holy One of God' even the 'Son of God' (Matthew 8:29). This one feared that Jesus would destroy him and the man in his power. Everyone heard its strange testimony to Jesus.

Jesus distinguished between the man and the demon. 'Silence!' 'Come out of him!' There was a loud scream and a convulsing spasm – but the demon left and the man was delivered. This was new teaching with authority behind it. To the people, the most astonishing thing of all was that the demons obeyed him. There had been no magic formula. Here was the raw power of the Holy Spirit, proving that the Kingdom of God had already come (Matthew 12:27,28).

By word of mouth the news spread like wildfire.

Peter's mother-in-law just one of many healed
Matthew 8:14-17, Mark 1:29-34, Luke 4:38-41

Immediately after that synagogue service, Jesus' authority was seen in action over the realm of disease and sickness. Peter and Andrew lived together in Peter's house in Capernaum with Peter's wife and mother-in-law. His mother in law was burning with fever, but Jesus ordered the fever to leave and at his touch on her hand she instantly recovered.

When the Sabbath ended at sunset, people were free to bring to Jesus all sorts of needy folk. They came in a steady stream until it seemed the whole city was at the door of Peter's house. As they passed by in procession Jesus healed every one, displaying a self-authenticating, attractive and uncontainable authority. Demons, knowing who he was, were forbidden to speak. They posed no problem to him and could not neutralise his power. But Jesus did not wish to receive or endorse their testimony. Their words could be twisted, and could so easily complicate the standing of Jesus with the authorities, who were very quick to accuse him with being in league with them.

The announcement to tour Galilee
Mark 1:35-39, Luke 4:42-44, compare **Matthew 4:23-25**

While it was still dark, Jesus went off alone sometime between 3 and 6 a.m. He saw the need to be physically recharged and spiritually focused. He handled popularity by prayer to the Father, aware that it could be a snare if it shaped his agenda. Comfort and complacency could so easily supplant duty. The opinions of his friends were not his guide. Simon certainly thought that he was losing precious opportunities. So he and a group hunted for Jesus to bring him back to his house.

Jesus was indeed a 'people' person, but had no wish to be impeded by them. Above all else he was the Son of the Father. And as well as having a long term plan, the Father had an immediate plan for Jesus which was revealed to him through prayer. In this instance he knew that the Father's will for the immediate future was a preaching tour of Galilee and not continued healings in Capernaum. So he left Capernaum to tour Galilee's villages with his call for repentance coupled with a ministry of deliverance from demons. He was confirming the arrival of the kingdom.

The healing of a man with leprosy
Matthew 8:2-4, Mark 1:40-45, Luke 5:12-16

Committed to the task of preaching in the villages rather than healing in the town, Jesus met a man who got on his knees before him. He had been discriminated against because of his skin problem, declared unclean and ostracised. This man did not question Jesus' ability; he actually affirmed it – but in the light of Jesus' priorities the issue to him was whether Jesus would be willing. We are told that Jesus expressed powerful emotion, first when touching the man, and later when giving the command to report to the priests.

Compassion was a strong power and Jesus was infused with it. He could not look on human weakness, disease and death without sympathy. His heart was open. He was the model and personification of kind-heartedness. This answered the question about his willingness.

He would be concerned for the crowds in their anxiety and helplessness (Matthew 9:36), when they were ill (Matthew 14:14) and hungry (Matthew 15:32). He was moved emotionally by those who had lost their sight (Matthew 20:34), by the plight of the bereaved widow (Luke 7:13) and by that of a boy who because of demon possession was in danger of self-harm (Mark 9:22). He would incorporate the idea in his teaching – as when the king had compassion on the debtor (Matthew 18:27), the Samaritan on the injured victim (Luke 10:33) and the father on his repentant son (Luke 15:20).

And compassion it was that ruled in this case as he healed the man with a touch. The priority of proclaiming the kingdom did not exclude healing. But in order to keep the excitement down that could have detracted from his ministry, Jesus issued a strong prohibition to the man against talking about it publicly. Reporting the healing to the priests could not be avoided – without their formal testimony those with a history of leprosy would not be received as officially clean. But the man could not contain his enthusiasm.

The net result was that Jesus sought more seclusion and accrued even more popularity.

The healing of a man who was paralysed: Jesus' authority to forgive sins
Matthew 9:1-8, Mark 2:1-12, Luke 5:17-26

Back at Capernaum he was far more popular now than he had ever been in Nazareth. His purpose was still to teach and preach the word. A good number of teachers of the law and Pharisees had converged on Capernaum from all over Galilee, some having travelled up from Jerusalem, 80 or 90 miles to the south. The teaching session was interrupted by four friends who carried a paralysed man, and who were escorted probably by several more. He presumably had come for healing, but there was no immediate healing from Jesus. He was about to hear a word addressed to him personally, a blessed announcement of pardon. 'Son, your sins are forgiven.'

This was Jesus' concern. But if the pardon was to be in any sense real, the statement itself needed to be valid. And for the statement to be valid it had to come from someone whose business it was to forgive and who was telling the truth when he said he had the authority to forgive.

Forgiveness is in relation to sins. Jesus was not talking of bad habits (that may be cured by a solemn resolve), personality defects (that may be improved by social therapy) or even conscious faults and failings (that can be corrected by apologies and the cultivation of good relationships). Sins can only be dealt with by being forgiven. It is humanity's universal and ongoing need.

Sin is anything that falls short of God's standard, or anything that transgresses God's law. It can be either active disobedience or passive neglect. To commit what God forbids is sin. Failure to deliver what God requires equally is sin. As a race of sinners, we have all broken the first and greatest commandment – to love the Lord our God with all our heart, soul, mind, and strength, and our neighbour as ourselves. Goodness is defined in Micah 6:8 in terms of acting justly, loving mercy and walking humbly with God. Sin is always against God.

The man, being immobile, physically weak, frustrated, socially restricted and psychologically under pressure, might have argued that it was simply adding to his problems to talk about sins. But they were only mentioned by Jesus because he wished to talk about forgiveness. Forgiveness is not turning a blind eye to sin; it is the removal of sin from the sinner, like the washing away of dirt from the hands or the lifting of a burden from the back. It is the cancellation of a debt by the creditor, and therefore removed from the account (Luke 7:41,42). It is something done at a particular point which has ongoing blessings. It is the start of something big.

And such forgiveness, we are told, was activated by faith, the attitude of absolute confidence in Christ. The people who had faith felt they had to get to Jesus tearing down all the barriers in the way. It was an attitude that Jesus was able to assess and respond to.

But there was unspoken protest – a resistance as evident to Jesus as was the faith he had just witnessed. He perceived the scepticism and unbelief in the minds of the religious experts who viewed his word of pardon as a word of blasphemy. If forgiveness was God's prerogative alone, who did Jesus think he was? This would not be the last time this issue would arise. He would later say to a woman who anointed him in loving gratitude, 'Your sins are forgiven.' And the other guests would discuss among themselves who this was who even forgives sins

(Luke 7:49). The religious leaders on both occasions had arrived at their conclusion on the grounds of insufficient knowledge. They needed to know more than they did. But words alone would not convince them. Their unspoken accusation of blasphemy implied that he had spoken idly, that his words were empty. So Jesus deliberately shifted the point at issue to show he was not playing a game of words. He would prove that his words had power, achieved things and never fell to the ground short of their target. Therefore he told them to pay attention so that they might know he had the authority to forgive sins. Addressing the forgiven man he said, 'Get up, take your mat and go home.' The effectual word was proof that Jesus as the Son of Man had authority and that his word of pardon had been valid. He forgives sins. This would become a great New Testament truth in which to rejoice. Paul could say, 'In him we have redemption through his blood, the forgiveness of sins' (Ephesians 1:7; Colossians 1:14). But for the Pharisees it was just another bone of contention.

The call of Matthew
Matthew 9:9-13, Mark 2:13-17, Luke 5:27-32

Matthew, otherwise known as Levi, son of Alpheus, sat at the toll-gate on the great west road from Damascus to the Mediterranean. He collected taxes for Herod Antipas. Jews hated these men and classed them with sinners. It was the sort of job that gave expression to the evils of harshness, greed and deception. Jesus' call was sudden and sharp, but Matthew was ready. He had heard of Jesus and quickly responded.

He gave a great reception in his house to which other tax collectors were invited – who we are told were all following Jesus' teaching. The scribes and Pharisees were again on hand to comment about these questionable associates of Jesus. This would become a constant charge intended to besmirch his reputation (Luke 7:34, 15:1, 19:7). Well aware of it, Jesus didn't seem to mind. Using the Pharisees' claim to be righteous, he would make a specific point. He had not come to call such folk, but sinners to repentance. He was calling people to new spiritual life and away from sin – but those who considered that they were well, fit and strong would not visit the doctor.

The question of fasting
Matthew 9:14-17, Mark 2:18-22, Luke 5:33-39

A question that lay in the minds of the public also bothered the disciples of John. They wondered why Jesus' disciples didn't practise fasting. Jesus replied that bridegrooms were associated with joy not austerity and so it was with his followers. This would change in the future, however, when they would feel bereaved when the bridegroom was taken from them. It may not have been easy for the questioners to make the mental adjustment, but they had to realise that things that belonged to the old way were not appropriate to the new. The new and the old did not mix. The old worn garment was not strong enough to take the new patch. And wineskins that had already been stretched to their limit with the process of fermentation could not cope with any new wine, yet to mature, that would cause further stretching. The new wine of the kingdom must have new containers to hold it. But there would always be people who when given the choice would opt for the old.

Negative undercurrents
Matthew 12:1-50, Mark 2:23–3:35, Luke 6:1– 8:21

In promoting the kingdom of God Jesus would need to manage and deal with several adverse factors. We can identify at least four of these – controversy over the keeping of the Sabbath, uncertainty expressed by as great a person as John the Baptist, open animosity from the religious establishment and pressure that came from his own family and friends.

Controversy

The controversy with the Pharisees over plucking ears of grain on the Sabbath
Matthew 12:1-8, Mark 2:23-28, Luke 6:1-5

The hungry disciples, walking through some wheat fields one Sabbath day, ate the grain, thinking nothing about it. But it had been noticed. And it was contrary to the law as viewed by the Pharisees who were quick to make their point. Jesus defended his disciples. Their activity was as innocent as that of David who in the past had eaten the bread of the priests. And why pick on his disciples and not the current temple priests who in relation to their temple service 'broke' the Sabbath? Jesus pointed out the more serious issue in that the Pharisees failed to understand what their scriptures were all about. He quoted Hosea 6:6 that God looked for a merciful heart not sacrificial ritualism. But in making the point he also said that he was greater than the temple and as the Son of Man was Lord of the Sabbath. The controversy had begun. It would roll on, and get very serious.

The healing of the man with the withered hand on the Sabbath Matthew 12:9-14, Mark 3:1-6, Luke 6:6-11

The dispute resumed in the synagogue. A man had a paralysed right hand. With an accusing spirit, certain people watched Jesus. Was it against their law to heal on the Sabbath? They put the question to Jesus, who didn't hedge. Inviting the man to the front, he had a question for the people. Did they really believe that the law forbade helping folk on the Sabbath? Jesus held a strong view on this and their failure to reply served to underline their error. Wouldn't they rescue one of their own sheep from a deep hole on the Sabbath? Of course they would. Was a human being worth more than a sheep? The law he said was on his side. All he then did was to speak to the man with the paralysed hand. 'Stretch out your hand.' It was a deliberate and public healing. The man himself was probably grateful. But the Pharisees by contrast were filled with rage. Their system was being undermined. And so a political conspiracy began between some Pharisees and some members of Herod's party as to how to kill Jesus. They were playing the man and not the ball.

It was time for Jesus to leave. The work of the kingdom of God had to go on, and Lake Galilee beckoned. This provided a special place of retreat which Jesus and his disciples used for prayer, rest and private discussion. So when hearing of the sinister plot, it was there they went.

The retreat to Lake Galilee
Matthew 12:15-21, Mark 3:7-12

The Pharisees, adamant in their view, would not be convinced. But Jesus was not going to be deflected from his course either. Matthew, one member of the group, was particularly impressed and impacted at this retreat. He recalled that Jesus fulfilled what God had said through the prophet Isaiah (Isaiah 42:1-4). Here among them was the chosen, well beloved, well pleasing and Spirit anointed servant of God who would proclaim justice to the nations without any distasteful argument or street soapbox. His spiritual touch would combine a gentle sensitivity with an iron resolve. On one hand, as the one who always held out hope he would not snap off the bent reed or extinguish a flickering lamp. On the other, he would persevere until truth and justice triumphed so that he became the object of trust. Messiah Jesus was the new reference point.

However, the retreat was interrupted. Jesus' popularity was growing. Large crowds also assembled there from the north (Galilee), south (Judea, Jerusalem and Idumea), east (Decapolis and Perea) and northwest (the cities of Tyre and Sidon). Jesus had eluded the hostile conspirators, but had no wish to hide from the spiritually needy. Add the curious observers, serious enquirers and those wanting healing, and the result was serious crowd congestion. As Jesus healed and delivered people from demon possession, he discouraged all further publicity on their part. Numbers were not everything. But the crowds came in any case. The confession of the demons that he was the Son of God would be twisted and used by his religious enemies who could not stomach his Messianic claims. At this juncture Jesus saw the need for depth of commitment on the part of his followers. It was a situation that called for intense prayer.

The selection of the twelve apostles
Mark 3:13-19, Luke 6:12-16

So it was that on a hill not far from the lake Jesus spent a whole night in prayer during which a strategy was born. From the vast crowds by the sea he invited a select number whom he really wished to be with him. And from this group, twelve were chosen whom he described as his apostles or missionaries. These would be his delegates, sent out to proclaim the good news of the kingdom and to cast out demons. But they were not ready for that just yet, not until they had been with Jesus for some time. They needed to be instructed and to get to know Jesus himself.

So, seven others joined the four fishermen and Matthew: Philip, Bartholomew (or Nathanael), Thomas, James son of Alphaeus, Thaddaeus (or Lebbaeus), Simon the Patriot, and Judas Iscariot. The instruction these were to receive was not long in coming.

The sermon on the plain
Luke 6:17-49

It was at this point, after the selection of the Twelve, that Luke included Jesus' sermon on the plain. Some see this as an abridged version of Matthew's record of the Sermon on the Mount (Matthew 5-7) while others think it to be a different sermon. It does not matter. The main thrust of both sermons was basically the same: that Jesus' authoritative teaching was to be obeyed. Jesus was the focus of faith. Luke's version, like Matthew's, concluded with the parable of the wise and foolish builders which Jesus introduced with the question, 'Why do you call me, Lord, Lord, and do not do what I say?' (Luke 6:46). He was presenting himself to his followers as the alternative leader in what was largely a formalistic religious atmosphere created by the Pharisees.

There then followed two significant incidents. In Capernaum, a Roman centurion's servant was healed and at Nain a widow's only son was raised from death. These incidents focussed on the fact that Jesus was a unique, compassionate and authoritative leader who inspired faith.

The centurion's servant healed at Capernaum
Luke 7:1-10 (Matthew 8:5-13)

The centurion's servant was about to die. Some Jewish elders appealed to Jesus intently on his behalf that the man was deserving of special treatment because he had been good to Israel and had even built a synagogue. The centurion himself subsequently sent friends to Jesus with a revised request, and they gave a different and self-effacing message. The centurion on reflection it would seem realised he was not worthy and had no claim on Jesus. Jesus need not move from where he was, but simply express his will by speaking – if he did that, then the servant would be healed. The centurion made the point that he could recognise delegated authority when he saw it – folk obeyed his own word because he represented the higher authority of Rome. He acknowledged that behind Jesus lay the powerful concentration of Divine authority. Jesus was impressed. It caused him to comment, 'I have not found such great faith even in Israel.'

The Jewish leaders had taken offence at Jesus' claims. But now the door of the kingdom was opening wider in a way that was unstoppable. It was not the only miracle to authenticate Jesus. The same word of authority, coupled with compassion, was about to convince all onlookers that a great prophet had emerged.

The raising of the widow's son
Luke 7:11-17

It happened in Nain, a town a few miles southeast of Nazareth. The crowd that was following Jesus met a large group of mourners leaving through the town gate for the burial place. The deceased was a young man, the only son of his widowed mother. There was no other man in the family. Moved with compassion, Jesus trampled over all notions of ritual defilement and touched the coffin. It was open. He could see the face. As the channel of comfort he spoke to the mother, 'Don't cry'. As the source of life he spoke to the dead man: 'Young man, I say to you, get up!' He responded by sitting up and speaking. A deep reverence penetrated the hearts of all who witnessed Messiah's life giving power. They were filled with awe and praised God. 'A great prophet had appeared among us.' The miracle proclaimed God's presence and the news travelled throughout Judea.

The lines were therefore drawn. The Pharisees would intensify their plot to take Jesus' life. He had offended their manmade religious system. Jesus would continue to promote the kingdom of God as the channel of divine authority, compassion and life. He was no ordinary individual. There had never been anyone like him before. He has had no equal since. The record of his life is truly amazing.

Uncertainty

John the Baptist's question and its effects
Matthew 11:2-30, Luke 7:18-35

John heard the report of all of this from his disciples. He evidently still had followers who had not, like Andrew, transferred their allegiance to Jesus. The lifestyles of John and Jesus were so different from each other. John had never socialised much, whereas Jesus did – a lot. John was languishing in prison, and his future did not look good. And Jesus had done nothing to free him. To everything we have already been told about John we must add the fact that he was human – and human beings who have just themselves as company can get quite depressed. When that happens they need assurance. With that in mind, the question that his two disciples put to Jesus seems less surprising: Was Jesus the Messiah? Or had John been mistaken, missed him and if so should start to look elsewhere?

At that very time Jesus was engaged in the ministry of healing and deliverance from demonic power. So Jesus sent word back to John that there would be no more evidence than what his two disciples had seen and heard. They could confirm that folk were having sight and hearing restored, those who had been lame were walking, those with leprosy were cleansed, the dead were raised up to life and the good news was proclaimed to the poor. John was given good reasons to stay firm in his faith and not stumble or shift his position.

Jesus assured the public that John's momentary hesitancy did not suggest that he was a reed swayed by the wind. His rugged lifestyle was that of a prophet, but he was much more than that. He was in fact the promised Messianic herald, whom God in the scriptures had described as his messenger who would prepare the way of the Lord. In terms of his character and moral fibre no one was greater than John. He was the Elijah who was prophesied to come.

Jesus then announced that John's significance was pivotal. The era of the prophets and the law in fact ended with John and the new era of the kingdom of heaven began with him. It was the kingdom that was now the live issue. Folk like the tax collectors who had listened to John as God's messenger realised this and entered it, but those like the Pharisees who rejected him rejected the message of God. The kingdom of heaven was set to suffer rough treatment at the hands of its ferocious opponents. But those who belonged to it were to realise that they enjoyed a greater status and privilege than that enjoyed by John the Baptist who had announced it.

Jesus did not want to leave the fickle crowd with any wrong impressions. He and John were in agreement. The contents of the book could not be accurately judged by a superficial analysis of its cover. Any excuse could be trotted out by unbelievers to reject repentance. Excuse making betrayed prejudice and was worse than a childish game. They had labelled John, the unsocial abstainer, as a man with a demon and Jesus as a glutton and a drunkard. Both accusations were groundless. The important thing to both John and Jesus was the kingdom of God. Those who repented and believed were the children of wisdom.

The generally indifferent townsfolk needed a wakeup call, particularly those of Chorazin, Bethsaida and Capernaum. His miracles, Jesus observed, would have had a greater impact in Tyre, Sidon or even in Sodom. Jesus felt this deeply and would mention it again on the journey to Jerusalem. But in such moments of disappointment he resorted to prayer thanking his Father as the Lord of heaven and earth that what was hidden from the wise and learned was revealed to the unlearned. He would continue in that vein. What was needed was spiritual light. It was in that context that he made his appeal to those struggling wearily with the heavy burdens of life, with religion's demands and with sinful failure. If they came to him theirs would be the gift of rest. If they committed to him, they would find even more rest in the service of one who was gentle and humble in spirit. The yoke he gave would not be difficult to wear. He was the one who lightened the load.

Animosity

This developed from an innocent social event.

The meal at the house of Simon the Pharisee
Luke 7:36-50

Along with many other guests Jesus had accepted an invitation to dinner with a Pharisee named Simon. As Jesus was reclining according to the meal customs of the day, a woman stood behind him, allowed her tears to fall on his feet which she then dried with her hair. She reverently kissed his feet before pouring perfume on them. Simon noticed that Jesus did not react, and began to form an assessment. He was critical of the woman because of her sinful reputation and of Jesus because of his failure to rebuke her. For Simon, this cast doubt on Jesus' reputation as a prophet. But he kept his thoughts to himself and said nothing.

Jesus, discerning his unspoken thought processes, told Simon a parable concerning a man who had accrued a debt of five hundred denarii, and another of fifty. When neither of them could repay what they owed, the money lender cancelled both debts. Jesus presented his question. Which one would be the most grateful? Obviously, Simon reasoned, the one who had the bigger debt cancelled.

It was then that Jesus pressed his point. Yes, the woman of the town had committed many sins. But they had been forgiven, because in faith and repentance she loved Jesus. Simon however had not offered any welcome to him and had no love in his heart for the Lord. Jesus was returning to a basic issue here – people's attitude to *Him*. And when he gave the woman his personal assurance of forgiveness it caused a stir. The other guests queried this. 'Who is this who even forgives sins?' An old controversy was therefore being revisited. It had appeared when Jesus gave the paralysed man the same assurance of forgiveness. The Son of Man had not retracted the claim he had made then. He was persisting with a notion which made him the focal point of faith and love and the source of forgiveness, but which in the eyes of Pharisees was blasphemous because it was usurping a prerogative belonging only to God.

The second tour of Galilee
Luke 8:1-3

The dust of controversy had time to settle as Jesus took the twelve with him on a second tour of Galilee, accompanied by a considerable number of women who supported Jesus materially as well as providing evidence of his delivering power from evil spirits and diseases. Joanna (whose husband managed the household of Herod Antipas) and Susanna probably related their personal stories of gratitude. Mary Magdalene's case of demon possession had been severe. It was ironic, then, that this tour occasioned a serious accusation.

The charge that Jesus was in league with Beelzebul
Matthew 12:22-37, Mark 3:22-30

After Jesus restored sight and speech to a man, the amazed crowds began to discuss seriously whether he could indeed be the messianic Son of David. The Pharisees entered and immediately terminated the discussion by asserting that Jesus was in collusion with the demonic world. They did not deny his power but attributed his success to Beelzebul the chief demon. They were backed up by the teachers of the Law from Jerusalem. This was blatant rejection with a malicious edge.

Jesus pointed out that if demons were the ones responsible for casting out demons, then that would include the activities of their own followers, and such division was a recipe for disintegration. But if it was God's Spirit who gave him the power, the issue was bigger than they had thought. The truth was that the Spirit of God through Jesus was plundering Satan's domain. It was evidence that the kingdom of God had come. Jesus was not in league with Satan. And the time had come to take sides either for him or against him.

Jesus had by now on two occasions firmly and clearly established his authority to forgive sins – a claim which they had disputed. Now he was to say that this extended to include every sin but one. If they continued to say that he had an evil spirit it was not a sin merely against him. It was evil spoken against the Holy Spirit, equating the Holy Spirit with the devil. This perilous attitude because of its own nature was unpardonable. He reminded them that their evil words were the expression of an evil nature. Good fruit came on healthy trees. But they were like poisonous snakes and their words would rise up as evidence against them on Judgment Day.

The Pharisees' demand for a sign
Matthew 12:38-45

Some Pharisees and the teachers of the Law asked if they could witness a miracle as evidence. Considering all that had already happened, Jesus remarked that the one relevant sign was Jonah's time spent inside the big fish. The Son of Man would spend three days and nights in the depths of the earth. And because he was superior to Jonah and even to Solomon, Gentiles like the Ninevites (who repented when Jonah preached) and the Queen of Sheba (who took time out to imbibe wisdom) would stand as witnesses against the Jewish leaders on Judgment Day.

Jesus then told a parable to show that all attempts at religious clean-ups would fail if they simply created a spiritual vacuum into which evil powers rushed to intensify the problem. It was just like an evicted squatter who returned later to the empty property with seven more squatters. The irony was that blatant rejection of Jesus made a man seven times more evil than before, whereas Jesus had delivered a Mary Magdalene from the power of seven demons.

Pressure
Matthew 12:46-50, Mark 3:20-21,31-35, Luke 8:19-21

Crowds were becoming a regular feature wherever Jesus went and their needs seemed to be taking priority over his. Hearing about this state of affairs, his family felt he needed to escape the strain and eat proper meals or else he would have a mental breakdown. He was working too hard and often not stopping for food. So they travelled the thirty miles from Nazareth to Capernaum in order to take him home. When word was passed to Jesus that his mother, brothers and sisters were outside, he took the opportunity to remind the crowd sitting around him that there was a deeper relationship than the physical. His spiritual family members were those who did God's will. His brothers at this time did not accept Jesus' claims.

Clear teaching about the kingdom
Matthew 13:1-52, Mark 4:1-34, Luke 8:4-18

Entrenched positions would now be taken. The Pharisees would continue to challenge, oppose and resist the claims of the kingdom of God. Jesus would meet their rejection with clear teaching for the benefit of his followers. He would be unyielding in his presentation of truth as he made the point that the disposition necessary was that of the receptive humble child (Matthew 11:25, 18:3-4).

These parables given to the disciples expounded the nature of the kingdom. All three writers recorded the parable of the sower. Mark added two others – about seeds, that illustrated the life and the growth of God's rule. Matthew included the greatest number – the wheat and the weeds, the mustard seed, the yeast, the treasure, the pearl, the net and the householder. In these parables Jesus presented the kingdom as the agent of life that would be resisted and attacked. It was an internal rule in the hearts of his followers, and was worth any sacrifice. In its ultimate form it did not tolerate evil.

The parable is a word-picture that uses an image, event, character or story to illustrate a deeper truth, teach a spiritual lesson or apply a relevant moral. It was common in Judaism. Jesus made great use of it – his parables fill over a third of the synoptic gospels. His stories were set against the realistic background of everyday life, the home, agriculture or issues like justice, greed and love.

Jesus used them as a teaching device because he was a communicator. Told well they captured and held attention. Jesus was aware of society's spiritual deficiencies and that folk needed all the help they could get (Matthew 13:13 quoting Isaiah 6:9). They were also effective in clinching one chief point, and therefore suited Jesus' strategy of addressing basic principles that had abiding relevance. But also, the use of parables served to sift his hearers. The key to understanding them depended ultimately on whether one was a disciple. If folk did not follow him, parables would be of no help to them at all. Jesus explained that they actually veiled the truth to anyone with a hostile mind (Matthew 13:10,11). Those who had a submissive and teachable spirit would understand God's truth, whereas those who closed their eyes were at the mercy of their own degenerate heart, hearing but never understanding (Matthew 13:12-15).

The kingdom was the agent of life
Mark 4:26-29, Matthew 13:8,23-30, 36-43

The method of the kingdom of God was seed scattering. The seed was the centre of the story. Life resided in it. If placed in the proper environment it would automatically work according to its own nature. The man who sowed and reaped was not involved in between. Even if he slept the life principle in the seed didn't stop. The mystery of growth may puzzle the sower, but nature did not wait to work till men's understanding caught up. Neither did the kingdom.

In the parable of the sower, the picture changes somewhat in that the life that was resident in the seed was transferred to a person's heart and life. It was when the seed fell into good soil that it produced a crop. Good soil is soil prepared with digging and the introduction of good quality compost. Spiritually, it means a noble, honest and good heart (Luke 8:15). Now this is not what man's heart is like in its natural state. The preparatory work of the Holy Spirit was necessary.

Finally the life that was seen in the seed and then in the heart was pictured as residing in human society through the children of the kingdom, who had become partakers of God's life. They had a different nature – they were described as 'good seed' (as opposed to weeds), the 'sons of the kingdom' (as opposed to the sons of the evil one) and 'the righteous' (as opposed to those who cause sin and do evil). This was because their origin was different – they were sown in the world by Jesus, the Son of Man, whereas the weeds as sons of the evil one were sown by God's enemy the devil. The difference between the two groups may not have been apparent at first, but as they grew, obvious and fundamental differences became evident. The weeds had a temporary association with the kingdom of God, whereas the righteous had a relationship with God as *their Father.* They would 'shine like the sun in the kingdom of their Father.' Their final destiny was also different. Angels would weed out everything that caused sin and all who did evil. They would be discarded with sorrow and distress into the flames.

The kingdom would be resisted and attacked Matthew 13:1-23,24-30,36-43

In human society the notion of the kingdom of God has more often than not been rejected as a way of life along with the king's authority. Jesus knew it would be so. Opposition to the message about the kingdom was to be expected.

The parable of the sower teaches that it would be attacked on a personal level in the heart. The seed could be snatched away by the devil, deprived of nourishment by fallen human nature or choked by distractions from society.

The seed trampled on was not valued. The message was not understood. Its point was missed. This was so easily done if mankind's reference point was anything but God. Of course, the devil's activity was not perceived. He was interested only in stealing the seed so that it never would be missed.

If the seed survived the devil's activity, it could be threatened by shallow and deficient soil. The crucial time was therefore not the reception of the word, but the test that came subsequently *because of the word.* People who wanted it easy, who were 'disciples' in name only, would fail it. Many of them would turn back (John 6:60-71).

The seed could also be killed off in its growth. Secular society is positively unhelpful to the spiritual message with the way it engenders anxieties and focusses on pleasures and riches.

The parable of the wheat and the weeds was Jesus' warning of the dangers of imitation on a social level. Both Christian disciples and counterfeits would exist in the world. But in and of themselves the presence of the weeds posed no threat to the wheat – the danger lay in the attempt by the wrong people to remove them prematurely. It was sufficient for Jesus' followers just to recognise the difference and let God be the judge.

The kingdom was internal
Matthew 13:31-33, Mark 4:30-32

Jesus would later say, 'The kingdom of God is within you' (Luke 17:20-21). The parables of the mustard seed and the yeast emphasise the internal aspect of this kingdom in terms of *faith* and *truth*.

On two occasions Jesus used the mustard seed as a picture of faith (Matthew 17:20, Luke 17:6). The simple act of planting such a small seed led to phenomenal growth, so that the end result was a large garden plant. The New Testament teaches us that it is on hearing the proclamation concerning Christ (Romans 10:17) that faith is born in previously empty hearts. It also teaches that inherent in that seed of faith is spiritual life, strength, and fruit. In 2 Peter 1:4-7, Peter would make a list of the qualities: faith produced *goodness*, which God considers to be worthy of praise; out of that goodness emerged *knowledge*, the spiritual faculty of truth absorption; this resulted in *self-control* so that Messiah's disciples could stay unmoved by adverse circumstances; in turn the result was *perseverance*, the God given ability to stay the pace; perseverance led to *godliness*, even while the Christian is still in the world; and out of godliness came *brotherly kindness*, the family bond, with the apex being *love*, God's benevolent, unconquerable goodwill. All of this, Peter taught, resided within faith, and needed to be 'choreographed' (not created) by the follower of Christ.

From this rural picture Jesus turned to the domestic setting of a Jewish woman baking bread in the house using a piece of fermented dough which she had kept from a previous baking. She 'hid' this in the flour and kneaded it all together. Just like the figures of a bird, a snake or a lion, the figure of yeast can stand for something evil or good according to the context. Here Jesus stated distinctly that it was a picture of something good, even the best – God's heavenly kingdom. He used it to draw attention to the silent, hidden and mysterious activity of truth as it mingled with the human personality to transform it. A heavy lump of dough became light, nutritious bread. Something that had its own inherent active energy, when used in the right way, was the means of transformation. It was a picture of the laying up of the truth of the gospel in the human heart. The psalmist had spoken in such language.

'I *have hidden* your word in my heart that I might not sin against you' (Psalm 119:11, italics mine). That which is believed and received in secret permeated the whole being.

The kingdom was worth the sacrifice
Matthew 13:44-46

The parables of the hidden treasure and the pearl constitute a pair, reinforcing one point – the superlative worth of the kingdom of heaven.

The treasure hidden in a field was found accidentally. It seemed to be just an ordinary field at first, but what made it special was something that had been deliberately hidden away beneath its surface. When a man discovered this fact it changed his whole outlook. He now knew the true value of the field and from that moment on it replaced for him all that he had previously held dear to him. Paul would later say that in the Messiah were 'hidden all the treasures of wisdom and knowledge' even to 'the fullness of the Deity' (Colossians 2:2,3,9). The value of such treasure was worth every sacrifice. The kingdom of heaven was worth infinitely more than the cost of discipleship.

The parable of the pearl was slightly different in that the merchant was actively seeking something that was publicly acclaimed as valuable. It would tally with Jesus' own words in the Sermon on the Mount that we make the kingdom our priority. 'But seek first his kingdom and his righteousness…' (Matthew 6:33).

The kingdom is intolerant of evil
Matthew 13:47-50

In the Kingdom of God there is scrutiny and inspection. Jesus was using the sea as a picture of the nations of men, the human race, with its instability and unrest (James 1:6, Isaiah 57:20,21). The gospel net was immersed in that sea. There was no discrimination in the telling out of the message of the kingdom. Some fish would escape the net, preferring to stay out of the range of the gospel. The net however stayed in the sea until it was full. All kinds of fish were caught in it. It was then brought to land so that its contents could be examined. The good fish in the net were Messiah's true followers, faithful to the last. But the kingdom had no use for bad fish. At the end of the age, the righteous would be separated from the wicked.

All of these parables that Jesus gave to his disciples put the opposition from the Pharisees into perspective. Truth will always eventually triumph over prejudice. And the truth taught here was about to be followed by events that were a clear endorsement of Jesus as the Lord – over nature, demons, death, disease and disabilities.

Clear cut authentication

Matthew 13:54–14:36, Mark 4:35–6:56, Luke 8:22–9:17

The reinforcement of the teaching began with an evening crossing of the Sea of Galilee, the first of a series of significant authenticating events.

Lord over nature: Jesus calmed the storm

Mark 4:35-41, Luke 8:22-25 (mentioned earlier in **Matthew 8:18-27**)

Jesus' suggestion was to leave the crowd, and the most successful way to achieve this was by boat. Jesus chose his seat in the stern, arranged his pillow and fell soundly asleep. He was awakened by frightened men who managed to blurt out that they were in danger of dying. Yes, there was a storm; yes, the storm force wind had created high waves breaking over the boat; yes, they had taken in quite a lot of water already. But Jesus was more concerned about the men, amazed that their faith had been completely swamped by fear. So frightened, and what little faith! Then he spoke twice into the atmosphere. 'Quiet! Be still!' The wind subsided, and the sea was becalmed. The contrast could not have been greater. The disciples, still slow on the uptake, were forced to think. Who was this man to whom even the elements of nature responded?

The psalmist had indicated that it was Yahweh who had the power to calm the violent surges of the sea and its raging waters (Psalm 89:9). No man can control the weather. If Jesus was just an ordinary man, this sort of story can be dismissed. But if, as was clearly the claim, he is the Messiah, the Son of God, it should pose no problem. It would be the sort of thing we should expect of someone simply acting as the Creator God. Many of us today worship him as such.

But there would be more authenticating evidence.

Lord over demons: Jesus healed a demon possessed man in Gerasa Mark 5:1-20, Luke 8:26-39 (mentioned already in **Matthew 8:28-34**)

Continuing their journey they arrived in the territory of Khersa on the eastern side of Lake Galilee and were met by a wild and fierce man who, it turned out, had a long standing reputation as being demon possessed. Having abandoned his home life, where the best he could expect was confinement by chains, he now lived in the burial caves, where he could go around naked and not bother anyone with his bouts of violence or worry them with his moments of depression and self-harm. He had but one companion in this isolated place. Everyone else kept well out of their way.

He must have heard about Jesus already, because when he saw him from a distance, he ran closer to kneel before him and address him by name. What followed was by no means a normal conversation, but more like a confrontational accusation screamed at close range. 'What do you want with me, Jesus, Son of the Most High God? Swear to God that you won't torture me!' When Jesus proceeded with the exorcism, the man begged not to be punished. But it was difficult to detect whether it was the man speaking or the demons through the man. The demons knew they had nothing in common with Jesus, and even accepted his authority as the Son of God to destroy them. They voiced their fear of premature torment. Jesus, however, treated demons as separate existences from the human personality. He treated the man as a man and asked him his name. No name was forthcoming, only a demonic reminder given through the man that there was a great horde of them. Fearing the authority of Jesus to send them into the abyss, the demons begged to be able to possess the bodies of a herd of two thousand pigs grazing on a nearby hillside. Jesus consented. And the pigs perished over the edge of the cliff in the sea.

The man himself was delivered, and by the time the townsfolk came out to verify the swineherds' version of events, he was sitting quietly with Jesus, no longer naked and in his right mind. Because, however, business interests had a stronger influence on these folk than the kingdom of God, Jesus was asked to leave. They viewed such interference with suspicion. Not the man, however. He wanted to get into the boat with his deliverer. Instead Jesus commissioned him as a witness to his family. When his changed life occasioned the inevitable question he was to tell them how much the Lord in his kindness had done for him. The folk in Decapolis (the Ten Towns) were shortly to know.

A third phase of authentication was soon to follow.

Lord over disease and death: Jesus healed a woman and raised Jairus' daughter to life

Mark 5:21-43, Luke 8:40-56 (mentioned already by Matthew in **Matthew 9:18-26**)

Landing back on the western shore, they found crowds of people waiting, one of which was a man by the name of Jairus who came with an earnest plea for Jesus to lay his hands on his dying daughter. On the way to the house, there was what appeared to be a quite unnecessary delay. A woman, treated by the doctors as a medical guinea pig, had become the impoverished victim of trial and error. She made up her mind to touch the hem of Jesus' garment, but to do so discreetly. She had probably heard the country wide reports that a special healing power radiated from him which encouraged people to make physical contact with him (Luke 6:17-19). Anyway, as soon as the contact was made, she felt free from her chronic condition of internal bleeding. But what she did not expect was that the flow of power she had received would be noticed by Jesus who had become aware that healing power had flowed from him. He was intent on investigating. The disciples protested that it was futile of him to enquire, but he insisted that this deliberate touch of faith was different from the automatic and unthinking familiarity of the crowd. He was not content until the woman came forward and told her story. She had not anticipated such individual attention, but was to receive a precious word of assurance. 'Daughter, your faith has healed you. Go in peace and be freed from your suffering.'

That was all very well. But while it was happening news came to Jairus that his daughter had died. There was no need therefore to bother the teacher. With the loss of life had come the final loss of hope. But Jesus took the initiative. He was able, ready and willing. Ignoring the news he told Jairus, 'Don't be afraid; just believe.' It was another instance where fear and faith were put over against each other. So with parents there and three disciples, Jesus held the dead girl's hand and spoke. 'Little girl, I say to you, get up!' She stood up, walked around and was given a meal. This was not just a reversal of death. She was fully restored. Amazing!

If the woman had been determined in faith to touch him, then he was equally determined in grace to touch the twelve year old girl. Either way, contact with Jesus brought both healing and life. This was further authentication of this unique Person.

Lord over disabilities: Jesus restored sight and speech Matthew 9:27-34

It would seem that these healings happened next. Two men who could not see were able to follow Jesus down the street and into a house. They addressed him as the Son of David, and asked for mercy. Jesus established first whether they believed he had the ability, and with a touch restored their sight. This act of mercy was not for public knowledge. But the news spread all the same.

At the same time, a group presented to Jesus a man whom a demon had caused to be dumb. The demon was cast out and his speech was restored. To some this was amazing. But the Pharisees remained unmoved. They had not changed their belief that Jesus was in league with the chief of the demons. Authentication could call for faith, and even inspire it – but it certainly did not guarantee it.

Jesus authenticated to his townsfolk on his visit to Nazareth Matthew 13:54-58, Mark 6:1-6

The Pharisees' adamant rejection was mirrored to a lesser degree by the people of Nazareth. Jesus' teaching in the synagogue caused a mixture of amazement and confusion. There could be no denying his wisdom, but then the puzzle began. They wanted to establish the answers to questions like how he did what he did and where his wisdom came from. It would have been a waste of breath to tell them what we believe and know – that the Holy Spirit was the power, and the Father the source. They saw only a carpenter, whose mother, brothers and sisters still lived locally and who they knew by name. Mary was quite ordinary, as were James, Joseph, Judas, and Simon. It was on such a basis they rejected him. Again here was evidence that authentication didn't guarantee acceptance. Their familiarity with the prophets had bred contempt.

Their unbelief curtailed his activity there. So it was time to move further afield and widen his ministry in the north.

CHAPTER 6

The Third Galilean Tour and Wider Ministry in the North

Matthew 9:35–11:1, 14:1–18:35, Mark 6:7–9:50, Luke 9:1-50

The twin themes of Jesus' authority and his authentication as Messiah continued in his further ministry in the north, after which he and his disciples would set out for Jerusalem. This authority was delegated to the twelve disciples whom Jesus sent out two by two.

The twelve sent out in pairs

Matthew 9:35–11:1, Mark 6:7-13, Luke 9:1-6

The accounts in Mark and Luke are parallel, and refer to the third tour of Galilee's villages. Matthew, whose summary statement does not distinguish between the three tours, does however supply us with quite a lot of extra material – particularly in the area of the spiritual and practical guidelines Jesus gave his disciples concerning their mission.

Their mandate was clear. They were to proclaim the good news of the kingdom which included the requirement that folk should turn away from their sins. They were to back up their message with a demonstration of what the kingdom of God stood for, namely God's *deliverance* and *mercy.* They had no complex organisation or support group, made no appeals for money, but went in the clothes they were wearing. The crucial factor they were to assess was whether or not the message was welcomed. If it was, they were to stay put and continue sharing, but any rejection was to be treated as final and they were to move on.

Matthew gives us some idea of what went on beforehand behind the scenes as Jesus tried to impart to them his own heart of compassion for people whom he knew were spiritually aimless, helpless and apprehensive. Such sheep needed a compassionate shepherd. The disciples had seen this already in the life of Jesus, but he nevertheless spelt it out. *Compassion*, he said, should lead them in the first instance to the practice of dependent *prayer.* Changing the metaphor from pastoral to arable farming, he said they should direct their prayers to the 'Lord of the harvest' to supply enough workers to gather in what was expected to be a large harvest. Obviously these workers would be those who would welcome their message as they went out. In Jesus' mind it was the prayerful followers who qualified as the *appointed* ones, and Matthew at this point gave his list of the twelve apostles.

These were privileged to be *his representatives* as they went first to the lost sheep of the people of Israel. What they themselves possessed they had received free of charge; now they were to give out free of charge. They were to be preachers of the kingdom in a spirit of peace not abrasiveness. As defenceless as sheep among wolves, they were to have the watchful caution of a snake coupled with the gentle disposition of a dove. God was in charge. Looking ahead, Jesus envisaged for his followers a serious time of rejection, hate and betrayal. This called for *single-mindedness* coupled with *courage.* Just as the master would be reviled so too would be his pupils. But they were not to be silenced. God was in control, and he cared for them. No one could harm their souls. So there was a special incentive for all who would declare their public allegiance to Jesus and a warning for those who rejected. Remembering that the kingdom was a divider of men, Jesus appealed to his followers to identify with him in love and loyalty, taking up their crosses to follow him.

A spirit of compassion led to prayer. Those who prayed were the appointed ones who were to remember they were Messiah's representatives and act accordingly. In adversity they were to be single minded and courageous. It was on such spiritual principles that their mission proceeded. They discovered it worked. Success was their endorsement.

Further authentication

Jesus authenticated to Herod Antipas
Matthew 14:1-14, Mark 6:14-29, Luke 9:7-9

Herod Antipas had been the ruler of Galilee and Peraea since the death of his father Herod the Great in 4 BC. The Herodian family was a genealogical mess due to the many marriages entered into by Herod the Great. It would have been much safer to have been married to Henry VIII! Antipas and Philip were half-brothers, and Herodias the daughter of another half-brother Aristobulus. Philip's wife Herodias was therefore also his niece. Antipas had an affair with Herodias, his niece and sister in law, while at Rome and then divorced his wife to marry her. That divorce caused a war with the king of Arabia whose daughter it was he divorced and sent back to Petra. Herodias must have thoroughly dominated Antipas.

With the spreading of Jesus' reputation, Herod was thrown into confusion because folk were explaining Jesus' ability to perform miracles by saying that John the Baptist had come back to life, or that Elijah had appeared, or that one of the prophets of long ago had returned. Of course it was superstition that ruled such minds, including Herod's, who when confiding in his officials decided on the first of these options – Jesus was John the Baptist, who having returned to life was somehow controlled by the powers of the unseen world and therefore worked miracles now which he had never done in his life. This idea constantly irritated him, and he wanted to check Jesus out.

Of course, it was Herod's guilt speaking. He had presided over what was nothing less than the state murder of John in very dubious circumstances. Herod had ordered John's arrest, because John had consistently spoken out against his immoral lifestyle. Herodias was filled with simmering murderous resentment towards John, but

Herod's initial response was a mixture of respect and apprehension. He recognised him as a courageous, good and holy man. For a while he was content to keep him under lock and key. And when he ultimately sided with Herodias in her wish to kill John, his fear of the Jewish people took over, because they considered John to be a prophet.

The fateful day came for John on Herod's birthday when lavish festive celebrations were shared with Galilee's government officials, military chiefs and important citizens. Herodias, knowing how to achieve her ends, sent her daughter Salome out to perform an erotic dance to the delight of the men. It was not difficult for her to choose her reward. Her mother wanted John's head on a plate, that instant. The die was cast. Sad he may have been, but promises were promises. John, the man who was the voice from God, was silenced. When Jesus heard the sad news, he needed solitude. He would later refer to Herod as a fox (Luke 13:32), warn folk about his moral influence (Mark 8:15), and when he met him had nothing to say to him (Luke 23:9).

The point of the account was that Herod Antipas, though unblessed, was nevertheless impressed by Jesus.

Jesus authenticated to the disciples

The two issues which had occupied Herod's thoughts – *the power* and *the identity* of Jesus – were then incorporated into two related incidents that took place for the benefit of the disciples. They were about to be taught that Jesus had authority first over material things as common as fish and bread, and then over the forces of nature.

The Multitude Fed

Matthew 14:13-21, Mark 6:30-44, Luke 9:10-17, John 6:1-14

They had all resorted for quiet to a lusciously green and pleasant place on the north coast of the Sea of Galilee near Bethsaida, but the inevitable crowds soon arrived, some so eager to find him that they were there waiting for him. Instead of recharging his physical batteries with food and rest, Jesus with genuine welcome and real compassion found himself teaching about the kingdom of God and healing the sick till late in the afternoon. At that point the disciples frankly wished the crowd would disperse to the surrounding farms and villages but Jesus had other ideas. He gave them the responsibility of feeding the crowd even though their supply of food and money was hopelessly inadequate. They had no option other than obey Jesus' instructions, so they organised the crowd into manageable groups of fifty and gave what little they had for Jesus to bless. More than five thousand were fed with five loaves of bread and two fish with each disciple filling a basket each with what was left over.

This is the one miracle recorded in all four gospel records. And we are left in no doubt as to its significance. It was designed to get people thinking about the identity of Jesus, as the Prophet promised by Moses who was to come into the world (John 6:14). In Moses' time the tribes of Israel had been fed miraculously by bread from heaven in a remote place. Then it was *Yahweh* who had supplied their need through *Moses*; now it was *Jesus* meeting the need through his *disciples*. The display of Jesus' power was intended to encourage people to seek eternal life and to attract people to himself as the 'living bread' (John 6:26-35).

Jesus walks on the water
Matthew 14:22-33, Mark 6:45-52, John 6:15-21

This second recorded narrative continues to illustrate the same two themes of authority and identity. The episode began when Jesus sent his disciples on ahead by boat to the Bethsaida that lay on the other side of the lake next-door to Capernaum. When he dismissed the crowd he had an uninterrupted time of prayer until the evening. Darkness fell, a strong west wind arose, the lake got rough and the disciples, heading into the wind and straining at the oars, covered just three miles or so by three or four o'clock in the morning. In the middle of a storm and barely making progress, they saw an approaching figure they concluded had to be a ghost. In addition to being wet, exhausted and despondent they were also afraid.

The point being made was that the problematic troubled sea was no barrier to Jesus. He used it to get to the boat. It became for him a way. Walking on the water was the celebrated action of Yahweh, whose path according to the psalmist led through the sea and who forged a way through the mighty waters though his footprints were not seen (Psalm 77:19). This was the setting for Jesus to speak his authoritative word – 'Take courage! It is I. Don't be afraid' – which elicited an individual response. Simon Peter, testing the identity of the voice, wished to be invited to share that unique moment. When Jesus replied, 'Come', it was a test of Peter's faith. Jesus' query afterwards was not, 'Why did you come?' but 'Why did you doubt?' But this was not the only emphasis. The main point was that the watching group were about to come to a conclusion as to the identity of Jesus: 'Truly you are the Son of God.'

This confession of theirs makes us widen our approach to the incident. If Jesus was just a man, then the whole incident could quite naturally be allocated to the category of folklore; but the New Testament writers do not see it like that at all. John (John 1:1-4,10), Paul (Colossians 1:15-17, 1 Corinthians 8:6) and the writer of Hebrews (Hebrews 1:1-3) made far more astounding statements about Jesus, stating quite categorically that before his incarnation he was no less than the divine agent in creation, by whom all things were created and through whom all things cohere.

And if that is the case, then the reaction of the disciples to the recorded incident was not only understandable, but was the only one that was appropriate.

Jesus authenticated to the community of Gennesaret
Matthew 14:34-36, Mark 6:53-56

At the plain of Gennesaret, several miles south of Bethsaida, where they moored the boat, Jesus was immediately recognised and the word spread. Folk came or were brought from all parts of that small region for healing. By touching even the edge of his cloak they were made well.

Consolidation
Matthew 15:1– 6:12, Mark 7:1–8:26

Following this array of impressive authentication was a time of consolidation and reinforcement in which important issues were revisited, miracles were repeated and the truth restated.

The Pharisees were challenged over the issue of ceremonial defilement Matthew 15:1-20, Mark 7:1-23

Representatives of the Jewish religious establishment from Jerusalem voiced a complaint to Jesus over his disciples' practice of eating bread whilst ignoring the ceremonial washing of the hands. The authority behind this requirement was not the scriptures but an oral law, codified in the Mishna and known as 'the tradition of the elders.' The rabbis attached great importance to it, whereas Jesus did not.

The issue was sharpened when Jesus referred to the Scriptures where the prophet Isaiah had contrasted the traditions of men with God's commands (Isaiah 29:13). It was evident to Jesus that these Pharisees had set aside the word of God in favour of the oral traditions. After giving some examples, he called them hypocrites whose hearts were far from God whatever their lips might have said. To the surrounding public, Jesus drew a sharp distinction between the healthy inner life and mere externalism. The more serious matter was that of defiling *moral* uncleanness – and this originated in the human heart. No foods *per se* were therefore 'unclean'. The rabbis were offended. When his disciples asked for clarification, Jesus emphasised that it was evil human thinking that needed to change. It led to all sorts of unrestrained sinful expression – sexual sin, theft, coveting, murder, deceit, lawlessness, blasphemy, offensive speech and pride.

The blessing of Messiah was to include Gentiles

The lesson of the great faith of the woman in Syrophoenicia Matthew 15:21-29, Mark 7:24-31

Jesus left Capernaum for Phoenicia, away from the strain of popular shallow excitement, the suspicion of Herod Antipas and Pharisaic bitterness. But even in Phoenicia his fame was known as people from this area had previously heard him teach in Galilee (Luke 6:17). If Jesus had been irritated by the hypocrisy of the Pharisees and their externalism, he was about to be impressed with the great faith of a Gentile woman just as he had been with that of the Roman centurion.

It's necessary for us to realise that Jesus knew from the start that this woman had faith in him. When she asked for mercy on behalf of her daughter, her faith was not discouraged either by his silence or by the adverse reaction of the disciples. Nor was she put off by what seemed to be the most discouraging truth that Jesus was sent only for the benefit of the Jews (Matthew 10:5-8). The Jews regarded themselves as 'the children' and the Gentiles as 'the dogs'. She did not dispute any of this. She even agreed with Jesus when he said that it would not be fitting for dogs to be given the children's food. However, she made her point, with respect, that she was not asking for something that would mean others were robbed. Children, she said, often dropped food from the table, and she was quite prepared to take her place as one of the little puppies under the table. After all, Jesus had come all the way from Capernaum to her region and she was going to make the most of the privilege. She was not like a dog out on the street, but a dog under the table. From Jesus she was asking for crumbs that would not deprive anyone else. An impressed Jesus seemed to have enjoyed the verbal exchange. He granted her wish.

A man's hearing and speech restored in Decapolis
Mark 7:31-37

From Phoenicia Jesus made a roundabout trip to the east side of the river Jordan south of the Sea of Galilee, a Gentile region known as the Decapolis, or 'Ten Cities'. He bypassed Galilee as Herod Antipas was still unpredictable, and the situation was complicated by the fact that many people would have readily forced Jesus into a political role as king (John 6:14-15). The Decapolis displayed a distinct Greek culture though Jews lived there also. He had been in this region when he had healed the man in Gadara and was asked to leave.

Several miracles took place there (Matthew 15:29-31) but Mark singles this one out. Folk approached Jesus on behalf of a man who could not hear and who had a serious speech impediment. Jesus took him aside to deal more personally with him, a preparatory action to encourage the exercise of faith. This man could not hear what Jesus said, so Jesus communicated in a sort of sign language what he intended doing. Fingers placed in the ears would indicate they were to be unblocked and the saliva on the tongue that it was going to be restored to normal use. When Jesus looked up to heaven, it showed the man that God was the source of his power. His prayer was accompanied by a single word of command, preserved for us in Aramaic, 'Ephphatha! (which means, Be opened!)' Its effect was instantaneous. Impaired hearing and speech impediment were cured. Jesus commanded discretion on the part of the crowd. He was not just a miracle worker. But they could not be restrained; people were amazed.

The disciples warned about the teaching of the Pharisees Matthew 15:30–16:12, Mark 8:1-26

If truth is to be prized, then error has to be assessed and rejected. Messiah's disciples were not to be uncritically gullible. This is the rationale for what Jesus was about to say.

It started when a large crowd of over four thousand having travelled a great distance had assembled and stayed for days, many of whom experienced a variety of bodily healings to the praise of God. The compassion of Jesus again came into the fore when he wanted to see them fed before their long journeys home. This time they had seven loaves and a few small fish. As before, he gave God thanks, and distributed broken fragments to the disciples who gave them to the people. Everyone was fed and seven baskets were filled with what was left over. There was more food afterwards than before.

Following this, on a visit to Dalmanutha, a district to the south of Genessaret on the western coast of the Sea of Galilee, some Pharisees and Sadducees came to dispute with Jesus and to trap him. Their point was simply that none of his miracles showed that God approved of him. They challenged him to perform one that did. Jesus probably sensed the same sort of temptation that the devil had brought him when suggesting he made stones into bread. So he was clear. He would offer no such definitive proof because there were already very clear pointers, just like the red sky at night being the sign of good weather. Their failure to interpret the signs of the times was their problem; it was not a failure on Jesus' part. Cryptically he said that the ultimate proof would be 'the sign of Jonah' – this was a reference to his resurrection.

It was then, while crossing the lake again, that Jesus warned the disciples against the teaching of the Pharisees, Sadducees and Herod. He likened it to yeast, but found that he needed to explain what he meant because the disciples were not on the right wave length. They thought he was telling them to stay clear of these groups even when they needed food. But Jesus was not talking about that. Shortage of bread was not a problem, as Jesus had to remind them. Twice he had supplied the masses with bread. The problem lay with their faith, their grasp of spiritual truth, their understanding, their spiritual sight and hearing, and their short memory! And if that was the case they were vulnerable to false and pernicious teaching.

The 'yeast' of Herod was moral corruption. The 'yeast' of the Pharisees and Sadducees was an erroneous system of belief that was not interested in mercy, justice and love and was powerless to deal with bigotry, malice and the abuse of religious and political power. Pharisaic teaching had created a poisonous spiritual ethos, and if the disciples opened their minds to such damaging teaching, it would pervade their whole life just as germs infect the whole body and viruses damage computer programs. It was the mind set of Herod, the Pharisees and the Sadducees that would be responsible for the murder of the Messiah. His mind set and theirs were incompatible.

Back at Bethsaida a curious miracle took place which involved a man who it seems had two problems with his eyes (Mark 8:22-26). First, his sight was restored, but it then became obvious that the man also had a sort of double vision which confused trees and men. A second touch from Jesus cured this related condition. As well as being a blessing to the man himself, and further authentication if Jesus, it would have been an appropriate parable in the light of what had just transpired between Jesus and his disciples. It was not enough for them to be able to see spiritually, they also needed to see clearly without confusion.

New truth for the disciples
Matthew 16:13–17:27, Mark 8:27–9:32, Luke 9:18-45

Jesus followed up his warning concerning bad teaching by establishing core key teaching for his own followers. Several themes emerged from a proper understanding of who he was. These would be developed more fully in the remainder of the New Testament and constitute the basis for our Christian faith up to the present day.

His unique identity as the Messiah
Matthew 16:13-17, Mark 8:27-30, Luke 9:18-21

Jesus had consistently shown his true Messianic credentials by his deeds of power and words of authority that were all infused with compassion. It was now time for his disciples to positively assess and confess who he was. We are being brought back to the link between the power of Jesus and his identity.

They were in the villages near the town of Caesarea Philippi way north of the Sea of Galilee. Jesus had just finished a personal time of prayer when he broached the matter. It was well known that folk had a range of ideas – that he the Son of Man was John the Baptist, Elijah, Jeremiah or some other prophet raised from the dead. But it did not matter much what other people thought. What was of consequence was his disciples' grasp of the issue. This prompted his question, 'What about you? Who do you say I am?' Peter immediately confessed his conviction that Jesus was the Messiah, the Son of the living God. Jesus replied that he had not only spoken truly, but it was truth that was revealed to him directly by the Father. It was not dependent on second hand information gleaned from what others believed. Everyone needed similar illumination to be able to know certainly, so it was not necessary for them to go around spreading this information. The unthinking crowd were only interested in their own notion of Messiah anyway. The work of the Holy Spirit was essential.

His victorious and vibrant community – the inevitability of Jesus' church
Matthew 16:18-20

The Father hath revealed one truth to Simon Peter, and Jesus would now add another. But first, Jesus addressed him by his nickname 'Peter' and commended him – 'You're a rock.' To confess Jesus as Messiah and

Son of the Living God, as Peter had done, was to be the basis of faith. As a foundation to a building, this confession would undergird Jesus' own distinctive Messianic community, his church, later to be described as a great spiritual household, a chosen race, a royal priesthood and a holy nation (1 Peter 2:5-9). The future of this international family was guaranteed. Death and all the powers of the unseen world would never prevail. Jesus would even go down into death but the gates of death and hades could not keep Him confined and neither would they imprison his community.

Then, by contrast, Jesus shifted the focus: this community could be entered because Jesus spoke of keys which at that moment were in his possession, but which were to be given to his church for them to open doors. Peter was not to be installed as the gatekeeper at 'the pearly gates', but he was to use 'the keys of the kingdom of heaven' while he lived on earth. And he did. On the day of Pentecost the door was opened to the Jews, later to the Samaritans and then to the Romans. And Peter was involved each time. A key both forbids and permits – believers are welcomed but the unrepentant are locked out. And through the proclamation of Messiah Jesus as the Son of the Living God, God's will that was done in heaven would be done on earth.

His specific mission – the necessity of Messiah's death and resurrection
Matthew 16:21-23, Mark 8:31-33, Luke 9:22

On three occasions Jesus spoke about his approaching death and resurrection. The path to glory lay through his suffering, rejection and death. There was no other way. He as the Son of Man *must* suffer, be rejected and be killed. This would be at the hands of the leaders of Judaism, the elders, chief priests and teachers of the law. As they inflicted pain on him and officially and finally repudiated him as the Messiah they would inadvertently play their part in the fulfilment of His mission in relation to mankind.

Peter for one could not tolerate this thought. But as he began to censure Jesus, Jesus turned the tables on him. He was talking like the adversary, speaking his own thoughts and not expressing the will of

God. There was going to be just one way for sinners to be freed from the power of Satan and the power of sin. Jesus told Nicodemus that 'the Son of Man must be lifted up' as the specific object of faith. And Jesus equally must be raised from the dead. The seed must die before it brings forth a new harvest.

This was so vital that Jesus would repeat and emphasise this teaching (Matthew 17:22-23, Mark 9:30-32 and Luke 9:44-45). It expressed his single minded focus and was a continuous line of truth they really had to grasp. It was central and can never be emphasised enough. They were not to forget what he said. The Son of Man was about to be handed over to the dictates of a human court, to those who had decided they would kill him; but on the third day after death he would be raised to life.

The disciples, however, were not in the right spiritual state to understand. They became despondent, confused and apprehensive and opted not to talk about it.

His stringent demands – the imperative of discipleship
Matthew 16:24-27, Mark 8:34-37, Luke 9:23-26

Jesus however insisted on talking about it. It impacted on his teaching about discipleship. Again using the word 'must', there were certain essential principles his followers had to take on board deliberately. Those principles he first applied in his own life and also in those of any would be disciple.

To the crowd and his disciples he underlined the importance of making a deliberate and daily choice. There would be no salvation without discipleship. His disciples must love him and unashamedly own him. Jesus had to be chosen and followed sacrificially and consistently despite the practical inconvenience to one's own selfish plans. This may well have involved material loss as God's purposes impacted on one's life in the world, but a man gained nothing by trading in his life in the interests of materialism. It was not a good deal, and it didn't work the other way. Nothing could be traded back to regain life.

Rather, those who lived sacrificially in the interests of Jesus and his good news would discover the secret of life. There was the possibility of potential shame attached to this lifestyle, yes; so Jesus warned against it. If anyone was ashamed of him and his words, the Son of Man would be ashamed of him at his second coming in glory. As we get older, facing the prospect of our earthly demise, such teaching embodies real spiritual power. The fact that Jesus will come again in his Father's glory constitutes our hope and motivation in this life. Paul was very clear about it. The children of God are graciously made God's heirs and co-heirs with Messiah, and as a matter of choice they share in his sufferings so that they may also share in his glory. Paul reckoned that any present suffering for Messiah was peanuts in comparison with the glory to be revealed in us (Romans 8:17-18). Self-denial out of love for Christ was the way of glory. Self-preservation would forfeit all.

His spiritual kingdom – the coming of the kingdom in that generation
Matthew 16:28, Mark 9:1, Luke 9:27

In the same way that Simeon had been told by the Holy Spirit that he would not die till he had seen the Messiah, so Jesus announced that certain members of his audience would not die till they witnessed the coming of God's kingdom, inaugurated by Messiah in power. He could not have been referring to his second coming because he said that no one knew when that would be (Mark 13:32, Matthew 24:36).

He had already told Nicodemus that no one could 'see the kingdom of God' unless born from above with the special activity of the Holy Spirit (John 3:3,5). He also made the point that when he expelled demons through the Spirit of God, it was a sign that the kingdom of God was come (Matthew 12:28). The kingdom was not a political, geographical or socio-economic system but a firm set of values invested in the Holy Spirit, especially the values of righteousness, peace and joy (Romans 14:17). And his promise to those who were listening to him then was that in their lifetime they would witness the start of that kingdom.

I have no doubt at all that Jesus was referring to the great day of Pentecost, when his disciples would be clothed 'with power from on high' (Luke 24:49). He had promised them (John 14:18-20) that he was not going to leave them as bereaved orphans but would come to them in the person of the Holy Spirit. This was both a fulfilment of Messiah's mission and a foretaste of the great glory yet to be at the second advent of Jesus. Yes, the kingdom of God was already present even then in the hearts of men. But the birth of his church as the next stage and his return in glory as the final stage were all part of the package, as then yet to be fulfilled.

His Messianic glory – the reality of glory linked to his 'Exodus' Matthew 17:1-13, Mark 9:2-13, Luke 9:28-36

In the account of what we know as the transfiguration of Jesus, a number of the preceding themes are continued and loose ends tidied up. Jesus took Peter, John and James up to a mountain to pray. It was as he was praying that his facial appearance changed and his clothes became radiant as if exuding lightning. God's truth would be taught in the atmosphere of prayer. It woke the three men up. After the episode, they kept what they had seen to themselves. As Jesus had intimated at Caesarea Philippi, no amount of human testimony could replace the need for Divine revelation through the Holy Spirit.

A comparison had also previously been made between Jesus and some of the great OT characters. This too is taken up when two men appeared, identified as Moses and Elijah, and talked with Jesus. Moses and Elijah were the last two names mentioned in our Old Testament (Malachi 4:4-6). The two seemed to share and reflect the glorious splendour that belonged to Jesus. Just as the men were leaving, Peter suggested that the situation be preserved. Then the voice that came from the cloud, similar to that heard at Jesus' baptism, confirmed to Peter what Peter had already confessed at Caesarea Philippi: 'This is my Son, whom I love; with him I am well pleased. Listen to him!' Jesus as the Messiah was the one with the authority – greater than Moses and greater than Elijah. Peter's suggestion of putting up three shelters (which would have given Jesus, Moses and Elijah equal status) was interrupted by the Father's voice from the enveloping cloud.

Jesus had previously spoken about the necessity of his own death and the challenge of discipleship. Luke tells us that the topic of conversation between Jesus, Moses and Elijah was 'his departure' (literally his 'exodus') which he was about to bring to fulfilment at Jerusalem. The wording means that this was something he was controlling.

Here then was a glorious and a suffering Messiah witnessed to by the two significant representatives of the law and the prophets. The New Testament teaches that Jesus' glory was multi-faceted. He himself would speak of his *essential* glory, the glory he had with the Father before the world began and that belonged to him because of who he was – someone who was the only begotten of the Father (John 17). In the gospel records we have encountered His *manifested* glory, demonstrated through his miracles. Added to all this would be an *acquired* glory, the glory of his redemptive achievements, for after suffering death he was to be 'crowned with glory and honour' in his resurrection (Hebrews 2:9). The whole Messianic program involved a suffering Messiah who through suffering would enter his glory (Luke 24:26). Jesus found it necessary to keep bringing this fact to the attention of his followers. It is the core of the Christian message.

The disciples did not understand Jesus' talk of resurrection. Instead, having seen Moses and Elijah, their minds were cluttered with questions of dogma such as why it was that the teachers of the Law taught that Elijah was to come first. This was based on Malachi 4:5. Jesus cleared their confusion. He first confirmed the content of that text – the promise was indeed that Elijah would prepare the way for Messiah. But they were to put that alongside the testimony of the Scriptures that the Son of Man would suffer much and be rejected. And so the Elijah that was promised had in fact already come but hadn't been recognised. It was John the Baptist who was meant. He had been rejected just like the Messiah was about to be.

The power of believing prayer: healing of the boy with a dumb and deaf spirit
Matthew 17:14-21, Mark 9:14-29, Luke 9:37-43

Jesus and the three disciples met up with the rest of the disciples amid some controversy. A man in the crowd came forward to explain that he had brought his son for healing, but with no result. He was desperate because without any warning the demon could attack his victim with life threatening consequences. It was a long standing problem. Jesus was about to use the opportunity to teach a vital lesson concerning faith. By default the crowd was generally obstinate and unbelieving. And his disciples needed to know that their failure reflected a failure in their faith, which could only be remedied by unhurried sustained prayer.

The father's mistake was to mentally extend the failure of the disciples to Jesus. 'But if you can do anything, take pity on us and help us.' Jesus responded by pointing out that the problem was not in his implied inability or in the seeming impossibility of the case. The problem was with the man's faith. Everything was possible for the person who had faith. The father learned the lesson and presented that very need to Jesus.

Of course, Jesus with a command to the evil spirit delivered the boy immediately, completely and permanently. It was not without resistance however. But the mighty power of God in Jesus overcame all demonic resistance. In prayer, the disciples would have discovered God's will concerning the matter which would then be implemented by prayer. There was no substitute for prayer.

His wise discretion on civic matters: the temple tax
Matthew 17:24-27

The half-shekel temple tax was a voluntary tax for the maintenance of the Jerusalem temple. Jews over twenty years of age were expected to pay it. Payment was to be made in Jewish currency, so the tax collectors and money changers would know who had paid. When Peter was asked about it he indicated that Jesus was in fact in the habit of paying it. Jesus did not want to give the impression that he and the disciples despised the temple and its worship. But they hadn't been in Galilee for some months and their failure to pay it may well have been an understandable oversight.

Jesus observed that civil taxes like customs duties on goods or the sort of poll-tax levied by the Romans applied to folk who were outside the family. As His Father's Son he was therefore exempt from the tax to maintain his Father's house. But in order not to cause offence, Peter was to pay it – the first fish to be caught by hook and line would have the shekel in its mouth.

The requirements of the kingdom
Matthew 18:1-35, Mark 9:33-50, Luke 9:46-50

The kingdom of God made several demands of those who would be part of it.

It required *a humble servant spirit* (Matthew 18:1-5, Mark 9:33-37, Luke 9:46-48). Indoors at Capernaum, Jesus asked his disciples what they had been quarrelling about on the road. They were embarrassed. They had been debating who was the greatest. Such a concept, Jesus said, was completely foreign to his kingdom in which the servant spirit ruled and therefore the least was the greatest. Unless they changed they wouldn't even get in. Humility was essential. So as Jesus hugged the child of the house, he made the point that lack of humility was a serious issue in that it was a sign that Jesus himself had not been given a welcome.

It also required *a generous inclusive spirit* (Mark 9:38-40; Luke 9:49-50). John reported that he with others of the twelve had rebuked a man they saw driving out demons in Jesus' name on the basis that he wasn't part of their group. Jesus corrected such a separatist attitude. If anyone performed a miracle in his name it meant that he held Jesus in high esteem.

Then in the context of the possibility of offending others in the kingdom Jesus spoke of the necessity of *an inoffensive and compassionate spirit* (Matthew 18:6-14; Mark 9:41-50). On one hand, to cause any of God's children to stumble, to look down on them or to hinder their faith in Jesus carried a severe penalty from which there was no escape. Conversely, the encouragement of a believer even with such an insignificant thing as a drink of water would not be forgotten by God. In order to ensure they were not the cause of stumbling in others they were to be severe on their own faults, motivated by the desire to enter life and avoid the rubbish heap. Referring to the purification qualities of salt Jesus spoke of having the good 'salt' of friendship in their relationships so that they lived in peace with each other. The compassionate spirit never drove anyone away but went after the wanderer, as is evident in Jesus' parable of the one lost sheep out of the flock of a hundred. Finding that individual was a cause of relief and joy. The heavenly Father did not want any of the flock (referred to as the 'little ones') to be lost.

And finally Jesus highlighted *a forgiving spirit* (Matthew 18:15-35). Peter asked Jesus how often he was expected to forgive his brother – a question that was prompted by Jesus' teaching that if his brother had wronged him he was to address the matter privately between the two of them in order to win his brother back. Peter suggested seven times in answer to his own question. But Jesus spoke of unlimited forgiveness. All the members in his community have been forgiven far more than they will ever forgive.

He told a parable of a servant who owed the king such a massive debt that he could never pay – even though he begged for time and promised to pay. The master in pity cancelled the debt. In the following contrived scenario, the forgiven servant's attitude was appalling as he turned into an unforgiving bully. Finding one of his service companions who owed him a comparatively trivial amount he became ferociously threatening and physically violent. Forgiveness was the last idea on his mind. But mercy was the hallmark of the kingdom. And God did not own any who rejected it. Jesus explained why he required his followers to forgive continually. God's reign established personal relationships. All have been forgiven far more than they can ever forgive one another. The pervading atmosphere of the kingdom therefore is that of gratitude for forgiveness. Therefore failure to forgive excluded one from the kingdom. And if forgiveness was genuine it must be from the heart.

It was on such a challenging and powerful note that Jesus' ministry in the north came to an end. Enough had been said and done to indicate what he and his kingdom were all about.

CHAPTER 7

The Journey to Jerusalem

Matthew 19:1–20:34, Mark 10:1-52, Luke 9:51–19:27

Jesus left Galilee and journeyed south. The time had come for him to complete his earthly mission and then, according to Luke, to ascend to heaven from where he had come. As Jerusalem beckoned it was therefore with great purpose and resolve that he set out. On the way he would encounter the same range of human reactions that he had met already, both positive and adverse; he would expound basic spiritual and moral values, and have words that were relevant for the disciples, the Pharisees and the general public. The kingdom of God was still uppermost in his mind. Already announced and soon to be officially inaugurated, Jesus spoke at quite some length about the norms of the kingdom and how it was vitally related to his death and resurrection.

This part of the story occupies two chapters in Matthew and just one in Mark. Our major source for most of this material is Luke, whose ten chapters have some similar content to what had been written by Matthew and Mark about the earlier Galilean ministry. This means that the core of Jesus' teaching did not change. All the key concepts relating to the meaning of the kingdom of God were repeated in a different setting to a wider audience.

Typical attitudes
Luke 9:51–10:24

Indifference – the absence of any welcome at Samaria
Luke 9:51-56

Jesus travelled through Samaria, where the mutual distrust between Jew and Samaritan carried the risk of open hostility. Samaritans assumed that any journey southwards taken by Jews would be to the Jerusalem temple, and this activated their sectarian prejudice. Travelling northwards home to Galilee through Samaria was not such an issue. The crowds accompanying Jesus may well have been going to Jerusalem also. At any rate they benefitted from Jesus' continued healing ministry. But when Jesus sent some folk ahead to make some preparations, there was a distinct lack of welcome from the locals. They did not approve of the Jerusalem visit. James and John wanted to exact a bit of prophetic vengeance on them – but this only earned Jesus' rebuke. So they found some other village.

Excuses – the would-be disciples
Luke 9:57-62, Matthew 8:19-22 (included by Matthew much earlier)

On the way, in addition to the presence of irritable disciples, Jesus had to deal with folk who were contemplating becoming his disciples. One such was a teacher of the law who made his pledge to follow Jesus wherever he went. We do not know if he did or not. But it gave Jesus the chance to spell out the terms. Things had changed now that his agenda was nearing its completion. There would be no guarantees – not even of any rest. Foxes and birds were better off. At least they had dens and nests. Then when Jesus invited another man to follow him, he wanted to keep all his options open and would not reorganise his priorities. For him, family affairs exerted a greater influence than the proclamation of the kingdom of God. A third individual showed hesitant interest, but Jesus made it clear that just like ploughing a furrow the kingdom demanded perseverance. The kingdom of God had no use for anyone who would wistfully keep looking back with regret over a decision made in haste.

Commitment – the mission of the seventy
Luke 10:1-24

As well as the men who paraded their excuses there were positive attitudes shown by men of commitment who provided a refreshing contrast. These were a moderately sized group of around seventy who formed an advance party that visited every town on the journey. Their brief was almost the same as that given by Jesus to the twelve when he had sent them through Galilee. There were some notable differences, however. Then, the twelve had been told not to go to Gentile or Samaritan territory, as their mission was restricted to the lost sheep of Israel. This was no longer the case.

As he had done previously with the twelve, Jesus gave them clear instructions: they were to depend on God for material things, praying that he would bless their work with more workers as folk were influenced. They should have no illusions; their mission of peace would make them as vulnerable as lambs among wolves, and in proclaiming the kingdom some communities would not welcome them – in the same way that the towns of Korazin, Bethsaida and Capernaum had not responded to Jesus. If and when they and their message were rejected their consolation was that they were in good company. The true disciple represented Messiah who represented God the Father.

In fact they were successful. And in good spirits they reported back that they had personally witnessed the submission of demonic powers to the name of Jesus. The authority delegated to them had been effective. Jesus who had been with them in spirit viewed it as a major element in the defeat of Satan. In it all, however, they were not to forget that the source of all joy was the fact that their names were recorded in heaven, and Jesus himself, moved by the Holy Spirit, gave expression to his joyful praise. The Father was fulfilling the plan, reserving his right to conceal as well as reveal. To be naturally 'wise and learned' did not constitute an automatic qualification. It was the spiritual infants like the seventy who got the revelation. So they were to know that it was a real honour for them to know Jesus, the agent of all such revelation. Little children they might be, but they were better off than prophets and kings who had not seen or heard what they had been privileged to witness.

Spiritual priorities
Luke 10:25–11:36

On this journey south Jesus expounded some core spiritual values. The lessons were given in various ways, sometimes in a parable he told, or a comment about an attitude that was expressed or in some deliberate direct teaching.

The need for compassion and practical love
Luke 10:25-37 – *the parable of the caring Samaritan*

A teacher of the law inquired how he may get eternal life. But he was not sincere. He was trying to catch Jesus out publicly in order to discredit him. Jesus saw the trap, and avoiding the question met it with one of his own. He asked the man about the way he read the law. The man quoted the commandments of scripture. 'Love the Lord your God with all your heart and with all your soul and with all your strength and with all your mind; and, Love your neighbour as yourself.' Jesus acknowledged that as a good answer, but knowing that nothing had changed in this cat and mouse game, commented that if the teacher could live up to that requirement then he would live. Jesus knew as we all know that no loves God as the scripture demanded. His answer certainly would have been different if the man was a sincere inquirer.

The man was losing the battle of wits. He had not caught Jesus out but he could not lose face either, so he asked a follow up question to perpetuate the discussion. It was the best way for him to justify himself in the presence of someone who obviously knew his stuff. Hence his question, 'Who is my neighbour?'

It's important for us to see that Jesus' story of the Samaritan was told in response to that question, and not the question as to how to get eternal life. It's as important to remember that it was given to a man who was insincere and interested only in his public status as an expert in the law. This story was designed to silence him, and silence him once and for all. It's a deliberately loaded story built on the mutual hatred between Jew and Samaritan. He had asked who his neighbour was. But

Jesus' answer shifted the responsibility to the questioner, teaching him to be proactive and be the neighbour. The priest and the Levite in the parable both continued their journeys, ignoring the injured man. But the man from Samaria got down to business. He actually went over the top in helping the victim, first on the roadside, then in transit on the donkey, and finally in the inn with ample provision for the future. There could have been no bigger contrast. At the end of the story, Jesus posed another question, 'Which of these three do you think was a neighbour to the man who fell into the hands of robbers?' Unable to utter the word 'Samaritan', the answer is, 'The one who had mercy on him.' At this point, Jesus drew attention to the fact that the lawyer had finally picked up the idea of mercy. So he told him to go and show a bit of mercy himself.

He did not say, 'Go and do this and you will have eternal life.' The issues had changed in the exchange of words. The point of the story was to expose this man's insincerity and hypocrisy. He should stop playing word games and start showing mercy, compassion and love.

The need to meditate on Jesus' teaching
Luke 10:38-42 – *at Bethany with Mary and Martha*

The two sisters, Mary and Martha, provided Jesus with an opportunity to make another point when he was a guest in their house. Mary took the opportunity to listen to Jesus while Martha was busy to the point of distraction with catering and serving. Jesus spoke in response to Martha's complaint that her sister should have been helping her. He pointed out that only one thing was essential. Mary's decision was to be commended. In choosing to hear Jesus' word she showed she was more concerned with what Jesus could do for her than with what she might do for Jesus. Jesus said that such absorption of his teaching was the disciple's supreme privilege, essential duty, distinctive mark and lasting joy. It is not without design that Luke placed this episode about contemplative meditation immediately after the parable about active mercy and compassion. It's not a question of one or the other. To force that choice would be as silly as asking a man whether he would rather have a heart or lungs!

The need for constant prayerful dependence on God
Luke 11:1-13 – *the parable of the persistent friend*

Inspired by Jesus' own example, a disciple obviously impressed with what he saw, showed a renewed interest in prayer as the secret of living. Jesus then gave a skeletal outline of the model prayer he had included in the Sermon on the Mount. Luke's version is much briefer, mentioning the priority of the kingdom, the disciple's need for daily food and forgiveness and the danger posed by temptation.

But it was followed by a parable about prayer that was set against the background of serving others, and which included the two elements of friendship and boldness. Prayer to the Father was prayer to a friend, and boldness in prayer was a strong element that built on that friendship. It was at an unearthly and inconvenient hour of the night that the man realised he needed more food. It was not for him, but for another friend, whom he would not turn away. But even at that moment his need for a special supply of bread was met. The point of the story was that the heavenly Father responds to similar determination, even if it may entail hammering on the door. He is the model Father who gives good gifts to his children. And his supreme gift, Jesus said, was the Holy Spirit, whom the Father would keep giving to those who kept asking.

The need for the ministry of the Holy Spirit
Luke 11:14-26

The charge against Jesus that he was in league with the demons was a repetition of an old issue that had first surfaced in Galilee and had not gone away. But no, the kingdom of God was not divided. Jesus was empowered by the Spirit of God, whom he referred to as 'the finger of God'. This is a rare but significant phrase in the Bible. At the Exodus, when the Egyptian magicians failed to reproduce one of the plagues, they concluded that the judgement was due to 'the finger of God' (Exodus 8:19). Also, it was recorded that the tables of the law were the direct result of the action of 'the finger of God' (Exodus 31:18, Deuteronomy 9:10). Jesus' authority over the demonic powers, mediated continually to him by the Holy Spirit, was evidence of the presence then and there of the kingdom and rule of God. He was overpowering his adversary Satan before their eyes and issued a warning to all who would resist him. The work of the Holy Spirit was necessary in expelling the demonic power from a victim, and it was also necessary that the delivered life be continually occupied by God. Otherwise the evil spirit, like a returning squatter, would bring far more misery to the empty life. This is why it is necessary that both the individual Christian disciple and the Christian community are indwelt by the Spirit of God.

The need to obey the word of God
Luke 11:27-36

When some encouraging woman in the crowd called out to Jesus that his mother was to be considered fortunate, happy and privileged, it was the truth but not the whole truth. Jesus widened her beatitude to apply to all who heard and obeyed God's word. However, in contrast to this group were the people who were continually looking for what they considered to be a conclusive sign. They would look in vain. The Son of Man himself was the only sign. If the queen of Sheba had been drawn to seek Solomon's wisdom and the Ninevites had repented through Jonah's preaching then Jesus as the Messiah warranted much greater respect.

The folk who thought they needed more proof were resisting the light they had already been given, which Jesus compared to the insanity of hiding a light under a bowl. To Jesus this was nothing but the expression of evil. The eye crucially was the body's lamp. But if the evidence it gathered was smothered by its owner the person would live in darkness. Each person was responsible for the way they lived, given the light that was shining on them.

Targeted messages
Luke 11:37–15:32

These messages belonged in three different categories: he would challenge his opponents, encourage his disciples and give general teaching to the public.

Challenging His opponents
Luke 11:37-54 – *the Pharisees and the teachers of the law*

Jesus kept up his challenge of Pharisaic religion as he majored on a person's inner life – and in particular whether he or she was motivated by generosity, justice and love. He had accepted an invitation to share a meal with a Pharisee, but like his disciples on an earlier occasion, had noticeably omitted the ceremonial hand washing before the meal. When his host showed surprise at this Jesus compared human beings to the cups and dishes that were set before him – it was the inside that mattered. There was no point in a person attempting to look good if he was consumed with greed, and there was no need for him to look good if he was generous in his giving to the poor. The Pharisees' practice of tithing was ruined by their lack of justice and mercy and their craving for status and recognition. It was a religion of death.

Listening uneasily to this was a teacher of the law who, feeling insulted by Jesus' words, had to protest. But as far as Jesus was concerned it was a case that if the cap fitted it should be worn. And it did fit. He forthrightly accused them of imposing impossible standards on the common people but never offering them any support, of deliberately keeping them in the dark and of being a hindrance to entering the kingdom of God. For them to have thrown away the key of knowledge in this way was an act of serious irresponsibility. Jesus had one thing more to say. It concerned the tombs they had built for the prophets. He did not see this as any sign of respect but as evidence of their collusion with the murderous motives of their ancestors. In Jesus' view such solidarity made them equally accountable for the entire history of Jewish persecution of the prophets.

The lines were clearly demarcated. And the opposition was to get even fiercer.

Encouraging his disciples
Luke 12:1-53

Broadly speaking, Jesus had two relevant messages for his disciples that are not restricted by time or place. First, he wanted to make them aware of what their real enemies were; and following on from that he urged them to maintain their spiritual focus. His words have a powerful relevance to all cultures including that of the western world of the twenty first century.

His disciples must identify their enemies (Luke 12:1-30)

The first of these enemies was *hypocrisy.* The hall mark of Pharisaic teaching and practice was a religious veneer that concealed a hard and evil heart. Jesus, however, was the same privately and publicly. What you saw was what you got. Not so the Pharisees. But just as daylight replaces darkness so the day of disclosure was certain to arrive. Truth will out. The hidden would be known. Things whispered in secret would be proclaimed publicly. Therefore Jesus called his followers to be transparent.

The second enemy was *fear.* Jesus saw that the threats men made to the life of his disciples could easily produce the desired effect of fear which in turn could paralyse all work in the kingdom. It was necessary to know that fear could be managed and Jesus showed them how. Man's threats were confined to this life. But the kingdom of God was eternal. God who was in charge of the afterlife as well as earthly life reserved the right to judge and would use that right, in the same way that rubbish was discarded into the relentless flames of the valley of Hinnom. So if there was any case for fear it was God who should be feared, not man. But there was no need for disciples to worry on that score. God their Father knew them, cared for them and would not forget them. The Holy Spirit would give them the words to say. So without fear they must acknowledge Jesus before men. It would be rewarded.

The third enemy was *materialistic greed.* When a man tried to involve Jesus in settling a dispute about inheritance, Jesus pointed out that his role was not that of a mediator in family feuds where the agenda was driven by self-interest. Jesus saw beneath the surface and warned against greed as a subtle and sinister menace which so quickly could dictate one's lifestyle and then dominate it. A man's life did not consist in his accumulated wealth, power, pleasure, fame or comfort. His true welfare did not start and finish in this world, but in God.

Greed is unhealthy, and growth without health is bad. A cancer cell grows. God focuses on health. Health may involve growth, but growth is a bi-product not an end. So in his story of the rich farmer, Jesus talked of two camps: those who stored up things for themselves and those who were rich toward God. There was nothing wrong *per se* in the building of bigger barns. The man's folly lay in his belief that greater material surplus equalled greater long term security which in turn would enable him to opt out of work, live at ease and feed his self-indulgence. This was his goal which he hoped to enjoy for years. But he was to lose it all at a stroke when he was to die that night and be forced to leave everything behind for someone else. The eternal realm inevitably and inexorably invades the earthly. For some that is a bright hope, for others a threat. The farmer in the parable had no spiritual resources.

The fourth enemy was *anxiety*. If the God who created the ravens and the lilies was their Father, his disciples should stop and consider. Birds found the food that God provided for them, and in Jesus' view not even King Solomon's sartorial splendour could compete with the beauty God conferred on the flower. So if his disciples made God their first priority they would discover his estimation of their true self-worth and see that there was no need to worry over food, clothes and the future. God their Father knew their needs and would provide.

His disciples must keep their spiritual focus (Luke 12:31-53)

Keeping focussed meant that they were never to forget that *the kingdom of God was treasure*. This was what they were to set their hearts on, not food and clothes. If they were occupied with the kingdom, the necessary stuff would follow. Their inclusion in the kingdom was the Father's gift to them among many others. In this context, they could therefore afford to be generous to the poor. Heavenly treasure did not run out, did not decay and could not be stolen. Satisfaction came with such prioritising because the heart followed the treasure.

Keeping focussed meant that they were to realise that *the reward of serving Messiah was fellowship with Messiah*. They were always therefore to be ready to serve. If a master, say, was expected to return from a wedding at *any* time, the servants were to be prepared *all* the time he was away, dressed for work, alert and their lamps lit. And on his return this particular master as the model servant would serve them. Being ready also involved making the property secure at all times and seeing that all the staff were treated with due consideration. This said Jesus was the sign of *faithfulness* and *wisdom*, two qualities that he considered necessary for leadership. And to ignore these would incur his greatest displeasure.

Keeping focussed meant *understanding clearly the implications of Jesus' mission*. Yes, it was true that he had come into the world to be a shining light (John 12:46) and a witness to the truth (John 18:37); he had come to seek and to save the lost (Luke 19:10) and to ensure his followers had abundant life (John 10:10). To these we must add that he came to bring fire on earth – a symbol that spoke of purification, light, warmth and power. John the Baptist had promised that Jesus would 'baptize … with the Holy Spirit and with fire' (Luke 3:16). On the Day of Pentecost this fire of the Spirit would be publicly ignited. But Jesus knew it could only occur after the suffering he was to endure on the cross, his 'baptism'. All of this would cause division in families. We know that Jesus as Messiah did in fact come to bring peace – peace with God, and peace among men. But using an antithetical form of speech he warned that in the context of discipleship and commitment there would be conflict. Peace at any price was not his purpose. Loyalty to him involved a commitment that may turn out to be very costly indeed.

Teaching the public
Luke 12:54–15:32

The public teaching concerned two themes: first, how to interpret and make use of the present moment; and secondly, appreciating that the kingdom of God was like a banquet.

The significance of that particular moment (Luke 12:54–13:35)

Jesus made some comments about peoples' view of the times they lived in. To understand and interpret events is useful at any time, but it was particularly relevant when such a special person as Jesus was in their midst. Certain things followed. Just as the sight of rising clouds in the west spoke of rain and a south wind promised heat, his presence among them at that moment was a sign and a portent.

This was a time for everyone to focus on and work for *reconciliation*, something that could be done without any official involvement of a magistrate or a judge. Jesus' words could apply equally to human relationships or to a person's relationship to God. All who heard him should take every opportunity to *repent*. A couple of current popular talking points concerned the Roman governor's outrageous massacre of some Galilean pilgrims and an accident at Siloam where a falling tower had killed eighteen people. Such suffering, Jesus taught, was not to be hastily interpreted as an act of divine retribution, but it was nevertheless a call for his hearers to repent. He followed it with a simple story about a fruitless fig tree, teaching that the present time was a time for some *groundwork*. There was enough time to nourish and fertilise the soil, so that the tree could start to produce fruit and therefore survive.

To give a strong incentive for faith as well as extra weight to these three challenges, Jesus demonstrated forcefully that the present time was one of *deliverance*. It was another Sabbath day at another synagogue when with a word of authority and the laying on of hands he healed a woman who had a serious curvature of the spine. This was an echo of the time in Galilee when he had healed the man with a withered hand. In indignation the synagogue ruler made his objection. Heal any other day but not on the day of rest. This got a sharp rebuke from Jesus. If oxen and donkeys were untied every day because the animals needed water, this woman's need was far more pressing. Satan had kept her bound for eighteen years. The Sabbath day was not going to stand as a hindrance to her deliverance.

Of course, to enter into the blessing there was a need for deliberate *commitment*. Jesus repeated two of his earlier parables, those of the mustard seed that grew into a tree and the yeast that transformed the dough. Faith like a mustard seed has to deliberately planted, and truth like the yeast has to be deliberately received so that it could permeate the mind. This was the essence of the kingdom. It wasn't going to happen by chance. Whoever was going to be saved was going to have to show resolve. Echoing what he had said in the Sermon on the Mount, Jesus advised, 'Make every effort to enter through the narrow door.' The door of opportunity would not stay open indefinitely. Once it was closed all efforts to enter would be in vain.

And rather ominously there was an end in sight. This emerged when some Pharisees reported a threat to Jesus' life by Herod. In reply Jesus indicated that his work would continue uninterrupted until his goal was reached. He would die at Jerusalem. In referring to Herod as a fox, Jesus then employed a telling metaphor about himself and Jerusalem. He had longed to gather her children as a hen gathers her chicks under her wings. But they were unwilling. Time would run out and when it did their house would be left desolate.

The past is what has come and gone; no one is guaranteed tomorrow; but we do have the present moment. Jesus' words remain relevant.

Lessons drawn from a banquet (Luke 14:1–15:32)

There were a number of lessons Jesus taught that followed in quick succession. This was on another Sabbath day at the home of a Pharisee. Jesus healed a man who had a water retention condition known as dropsy. Again, knowing that he was being observed, he did it intentionally to highlight the truth that *compassion* took priority over man's religious rules about a day.

He followed this with advice concerning *humility* as he noticed certain folk choosing the best places – on their assumption that everyone subconsciously or otherwise concurred with their view of themselves that they deserved the best. But pride, said Jesus, comes before a fall, whereas the choice of a less important place left room for an upgrade. If folk lived a humble life with God there was always room for surprise.

Jesus then had advice for his host concerning *grace.* Were banquets given as a *quid pro quo*? Well if not, why not lay one on for those who could not return the favour? God would approve. It was the sort of thing he did. It was in fact the essence of the good news. At this a sympathetic man at the table commented to Jesus, 'Blessed is the man who will eat at the feast in the kingdom of God.' Jesus had no argument with that. His only comment questioned why it was, then, that people made lame excuses for their absence. The parable he told of the man who bought a field, another who had just got married and a third who'd bought some oxen, underlined people's rejection of God's invitation to the kingdom. Their insult would feed anger, but it wouldn't affect the kingdom in the slightest. God's house would be filled. That was his purpose, and it would happen with or without the people who excused themselves.

At this point Luke inserted a reminder of an accompanying truth to that of the kingdom's invitation. In the light of the excuses made, Jesus advised his hearers to count the cost of discipleship because the kingdom required ongoing commitment. What, say, if one's family was antagonistic to Jesus? Or what if one's own aspirations in life created a conflict of interest? What would be one's decision then? Well, said Jesus, take those issues on board at the outset, make the choice beforehand and stick with it. Builders made their financial estimates before they started building; military leaders decided whether they would fight or negotiate because they thought ahead. Messiah's disciples likewise were to think ahead. They must give up their grip on everything but the kingdom. That, after all, was the treasure. So they were to renounce all other ownership rights and become stewards of the kingdom. Such commitment was its successful secret ingredient – as unique as the factor that makes salt what it is. Lose that special ingredient and you have lost the power to fertilise the soil and sanitise the manure pile. Jesus was being serious. People should take this on board. Those with ears should listen attentively.

Possibly in response to this last statement, tax collectors and other folk labelled as 'sinners' congregated eagerly to listen to him, which prompted the Pharisees and the teachers of the law to mutter again about the questionable company Jesus kept. 'This man welcomes sinners and eats with them.' Well yes, he did. But it wasn't the whole truth. Jesus was not lowering his standards as they had implied, but was joyously welcoming all *repentant* sinners. This was a matter for open and public rejoicing not one to complain about. So their accusation became the setting for three relevant parables (Luke 15) – those of the sheep that had strayed, the coin that had been lost and the reckless prodigal son who returned home.

The thought of one missing sheep out of a hundred impelled its owner to concentrate all of his efforts on finding it. When it was found, it was a matter for joy. The knowledge of one lost silver coin of ten urged its owner to sweep the house till it was found. Both the shepherd and the lady of the house then called friends and neighbours to share their joy. Now, if men and women were more valuable than sheep and coins, then it was a matter of undiluted joy when they repented and entered the kingdom of God. Certainly the angels in heaven rejoiced – in striking contrast to the miserable mutterings of Jesus' religious critics.

Having introduced the idea of repentance in applying the first two stories, the third story defined what it was. An insensitive younger son wasted his inheritance in a far country out of sight of his father and home. But things soon went sour, and from bad to worse until he was destitute. The only option then open to him was to repent, to change his mind, his values and his attitudes and see if father and home would receive him. He made up his mind to admit openly he had sinned in the most serious of ways. Desperately, he prepared a little speech to say to his father, which in the event he would not be allowed to finish. For his eager father was enthusiastic in welcoming the repentant boy, and threw an impromptu party complete with food, music and dancing.

Every sinner's repentance is thus celebrated in heaven. That was why Jesus welcomed them and ate with them. But Jesus had not yet finished his point. There was an older son who was also welcomed to the celebration, but who in anger refused to attend. He did not want to be associated with the sinner and preferred to stay outside in the field. Pharisees were given every chance to repent, but most refused because they were fussy about who they socialised with. By such fussiness they excluded themselves from the kingdom of God.

Kingdom norms

Matthew 19:1–20:34, Mark 10:1-52, Luke 16:1 – 19:27

Anyone who was part of the Kingdom of God needed to be aware of its implications and the impact it would have on one's behaviour and disposition. Jesus applied this to the issues of handling both money and human relationships, before giving very clear teaching about the nature of the kingdom and the practical changes it brought.

Wisdom in regard to money
Luke 16:1-31

Jesus told a parable of the dishonest manager (Luke 16:1-12) as a launch pad for some practical lessons. The wasteful manager in conscious danger of losing his job got cash flowing again by granting big discounts. He acted purely out of self-interest, but had however shrewdly used common sense in the situation. Jesus, far from advocating dishonesty, simply pointed out that the people of the world often display relevant common sense. The use of common sense for his disciples meant they were to use material wealth to serve the eternal cause. Money should be confined to the role of servant, and as such should enrich friendships. Unlike the manager, his followers were to be faithful and honest in the smallest of matters, for good stewardship in material things was good training for spiritual responsibility in the kingdom. They were not to allow themselves to be ruled by money. God was their one Master. They were to love him not money (Luke 16:13-15).

This was too much for some sneering Pharisees whose controlling factor was in fact money. Jesus reminded them that however impressive they appeared, God knew their hearts. And what humans prized so highly was actually detestable to him. Many people today enjoy lavish lifestyles because of their religious exploitation of the poor.

Wealth exerted no influence on a man's condition after his death (16:16-31). But the Scriptures did – especially those that were fulfilled when John the Baptist started to proclaim the good news of the kingdom of God. So, in the parable that followed, it was the rich man with all his money who did not get to heaven. He is pictured rather as a tormented, sorry soul pleading with father Abraham for the wellbeing of his family. And all that Abraham could tell him was that the Scriptures should be the controlling factor of those still alive on earth.

Healthy relationships
Luke 17:1-10

In the kingdom there could be no excuses for those who were stumbling stones that caused folk to trip up spiritually. It was a danger for all to be aware of and guard against. A second principle was that forgiveness was to be freely bestowed on the repentant, even if the same brother offended seven times in a day. This was linked with the need for faith, particularly the confidence that such recurring problems in relationships could be cured at root. Finally, all disciples were to persevere with their individual duty to their Master remembering that after all was said and done there would never be a time when they stopped being servants.

Gratitude to God

Luke 17:11-19 – *ten men with leprosy healed*

Along the regional border between Samaria and Galilee Jesus was petitioned by ten men with leprosy. He told them to report to the priests and as they went they were healed. Just one of them, a Samaritan, came back to thank Jesus and praise God. His personal cleansing meant so much to him, not least that he would be accepted back into society. But praise and thanks were also as important, so much so that Jesus made a comment. When the man gave glory to God and showed gratitude to Jesus he revealed a healthy spiritual disposition.

The Impact of the kingdom

Matthew 19:1–20:34, Mark 10:1-52, Luke 17:20–19:27

It was important to think clearly about the kingdom or rule of God. Jesus first stressed by way of introduction that it had two aspects. On the one hand it was a matter of internal personal experience, summarised by the phrase 'within you' (Luke 17:20-21). On the other hand it was destined to be the ultimate global phenomenon (Luke 17:22-37) at which the Son of Man would be revealed from heaven as visibly as sheet lightning. This, however, was not to be an immediate event, but would happen sometime after his suffering and rejection. It would be as sudden as was the Flood in Noah's time and the destruction of Sodom in Abraham's time. And of any two people alive when it happened, one would be overwhelmed by it while the other survived.

It was the internal aspect of the kingdom as the rule of God in the inner life of his disciples that Jesus was most concerned with. It tallied with the teaching he gave about a new birth that was the work of the Holy Spirit (John 3). He told Nicodemus that such a new birth was essential if anyone was to appreciate and experience the kingdom of God. The kingdom of God had a transforming effect in so many ways.

God's rule instils a continual spirit of prayer for justice
Luke 18:1-8 – *the parable of the widow and the judge*

The lesson taught here was that citizens of the kingdom of God should persist in prayer. Even the autocratic judge who was a law unto himself ultimately gave in to the widow's plea for justice when her only weapon was persistence. He came to realise he would lose any war of attrition! Like the widow God's people cry out to him day and night. Unlike the judge God would dispense justice speedily. The issue was whether each generation would persevere in such faith until the return of Messiah.

God's rule prompts a conscious sense of humility when praying
Luke 18:9-14 – *the story of the Pharisee and the tax collector*

This was told to show how any man was accepted, or 'justified', before God. The Pharisee was concerned about his reputation and the impression he made in public. His complacent mind set and misguided opinion of himself blurred all reality. Confident in his own righteousness he looked down on others. He compared his standards with those of other men and reminded himself of the points he thought were important, particularly that he had steered clear of certain vices and had consistently embraced certain virtues. He was scoring merit points. He was proud.

By contrast the tax collector came with a heavy burden, facing up to the knowledge of himself as a sinner. He was conscious that God was there and reminded himself of the one point he knew to be vital – namely, God's mercy. He was not parading merit, but pleading for mercy. He was humble. The Pharisee went away unchanged, presumably to return another time to repeat the same religious exercise. The tax collector went home justified, acquitted, declared right before God.

The kingdom placed the highest of premiums on humility.

God's rule challenges hard heartedness
Matthew 19:1-12, Mark 10:1-12 – *Jesus questioned about divorce*

There had been sharp disagreements already between Jesus and the Pharisees over Jesus' observance of the Sabbath day, his claim to forgive sins, the nature of the power source behind his miracles and the perils of formal religion. He had warned his followers on more than one occasion of the serious weaknesses of the Pharisaic system which housed a substandard righteousness, a worship that was no more than words and a substitution of human traditions for God's commands.

So when some Pharisees, reflecting the then current diversity of views, put a question to him about divorce and the law, Jesus was aware of the trap. He did not belong to the rabbinical schools of Hillel or Shammai or any in between, but quoted the creation ordinance of marriage in which a man and a woman were united together by God to form a new relational unit. Allowing that there were exceptions, the general principle was that man must not break up what God had joined. If a man was guilty of sexual unfaithfulness, or divorced a faithful wife, he sinned against her. It was a violation of the marriage covenant. And when Moses later permitted divorce it was according to Jesus a sad comment on the hardness of the human heart.

God's rule demands receptive trust
Matthew 19:13-15, Mark 10:13-16, Luke 18:15-17

It seems as if Matthew and Mark deliberately set the childlike in contrast to the hard hearted. When infants were brought to Jesus for his touch upon them, the disciples were annoyed. But Jesus used it to teach a clear lesson. The disciples' rebuke was one of those hindrances to folk wishing to enter the kingdom of God, whereas the kingdom in fact belonged to the uncomplicated and the unsophisticated. Those who would enter it must receive it like a little child. There was no alternative.

God's rule yields to no rival
Matthew 19:16-30, Mark 10:17-31, Luke 18:18-30 – *the rich young ruler*

A rich young man initially showed great interest, but then wavered and finally retracted his choice. He was interested in eternal life, had kept the social commandments from his youth and thought of Jesus as a 'good' teacher even though it was exceptional for anyone to address a rabbi in such a way. But for some reason his earthly wealth (for which he no doubt thanked God) stood in competition with his desire for heavenly wealth. If that remained the case, the kingdom of God must win the debate. It was the main treasure. So Jesus gave the man a promise that was contingent on his obedience to a command. If he were to let go of the material riches he would get treasure in heaven. The poor would benefit and so would he. But when he realised that following Jesus involved such a major social and spiritual adjustment he was not prepared for the emotional wrench. It was another instance of the proverb of a camel getting through the eye of a needle. As things stood, it was quite impossible. God must win the day and when folk surrendered to his demands, they would never lose out.

God's rule sifts the mercenary minded from the obedient
Matthew 20:1-16 – *the parable of the workers in the vineyard*

After the young man departed in sadness, Peter became reflective. He and the others had left everything to follow Jesus, and he was therefore wondering what reward they would get. Jesus gave a straight answer. When the kingdom of God was universally established as all things were made new, they would share Messiah's authority.

But Peter's question gave Jesus the impression that what was uppermost in his mind was the desire to be first. The point needed to be made that those who pushed themselves to the front would discover that they were sent to the back of the queue. 'Many who are first will be last, and many who are last will be first' (Matthew 19:30). The parable of the workers in the vineyard followed directly to clinch this point (Matthew 20:16). It was told to define two groups of workers that displayed two different attitudes of serving God. The first group agreed a wage beforehand, thus making sure of what they would get – a denarius for a day's work. This was the very attitude that Peter's question raised. Jesus used the parable to point out that such people at the end of the day could become envious, irritable and petulant, especially when witnessing the generosity of God at work. But the second group of workers were those who, at whatever time of the day they were approached, just did as they were told from that moment on. They obeyed without negotiating their fee; and they were blessed. The first set of workers would find out that God was fair and kept his word to them. But the obedient workers discovered something more – that God was generous. People who were attracted to the kingdom were not really bothered about what reward they would get. Some questions should never be asked.

God's rule repels status seekers
Matthew 20:17-28, Mark 10:32-45, Luke 18:31-34 – *the request of James and John*

Jesus emphasised again that he was to be handed over to the Jewish authorities who in collusion with the Gentiles would condemn him to death. He made it very clear that this was a unique time in which the prophetic scriptures would be fulfilled. He also made it clear that three days later he would be raised from the dead. This was not the first time Jesus had tried to prepare his disciples (see Mark 8:31 and Mark 9:31), but they didn't get it.

In spite of what Jesus had just taught in the parable of the workers in the vineyard, James and John had a question they were burning to ask. Their mother was involved too. The favour they desired reflected their selfish ambition. They wanted preeminent places near Messiah's throne in his glorious Kingdom. Their request caused dissension, indignation and resentment in the group. And equally serious, they had misinterpreted the priorities of the kingdom. The great ones in the kingdom were not those who exerted power or played the tyrant but those in whom a servant spirit had replaced the itch for status. And the Son of man was the outstanding illustration of this principle of self-denial.

It was in this context that Jesus returned to the theme of his death and resurrection. There would be no kingdom unless he died and rose again. He referred to his death by means of three figures: it was a cup he had to drink, a baptism he had to endure and a ransom he had to pay.

The *cup* (Matthew 26:39) was a metaphor for shame or suffering. James and John were told that they could and would indeed partake of these as did Jesus. But one aspect of the cup they could never experience, namely, the cup of punishment or the cup of God's wrath (Psalm 75:8, Isaiah 51:17, Jeremiah 25:15, Ezekiel 23:31). No one could drink that and hope to survive. It was this cup that Jesus knew he had to drink in order to free his people from the curse announced by the law. Later, Paul would teach that Jesus became a curse for them (Galatians 3:10-14). His picture was that when Jesus died he became a sort of shield *over* his people, sheltering them from the legitimate wrath of God against sin. And he would do this so that the blessing promised to Abraham might be shared by the Gentiles. This cup, Jesus told Peter in the garden of Gethsemane, was given to him by his Father (John 18:11).

The *baptism* he said he must endure was also a figure for his death (Luke 12:50). But it adds the thought of survival to that of judgement. The word was used in relation to both the Flood (1 Peter 3:18-22) and the Red Sea (1 Corinthians 10:2). The Israelites came *through* the Sea which engulfed the Egyptians. They were, metaphorically, 'all baptized' as followers of Moses. The account of the Flood also emphasised the two ideas of judgement and survival – judgement was poured out on the great wickedness of society while Noah and his family survived in a purpose built boat. Now, just as the ark came *through* the flood so Jesus would come through the judgment of God. The baptism he spoke of was thus a passing through death, to emerge in resurrection life.

And then Jesus referred to the sacrifice of his life as a *ransom* he had to pay. The ransom was the price paid for a slave who was then set free by the one who bought him. It has the notion of exchange. Jesus gave his own life as the price of freedom for the slaves of sin. We are bought with a price. Jesus delivered folk from sin's power.

It cannot be emphasised enough that the inauguration of the kingdom of God depended on Jesus' death and resurrection. Jesus knew it, but no one else seemed to get the message.

God's rule channels Messiah's saving and moral power

Matthew 20:29-34, Mark 10:46-52, Luke 18:35-43 – *Bartimaeus' sight restored*

A couple of miles separated the Jericho of the Old Testament from the new Roman town. Somewhere between the two sites Jesus encountered two men, one of whom Mark knew by name – Bartimaeus, the son of Timaeus. Blindness had cut them off from meaningful involvement in society and made them utterly dependent upon the pity and charity of others. Night or day would make no difference. Their hearing was good, however, and when they understood from the crowd that Jesus of Nazareth was passing by their thoughts took shape. Other men had had their sight restored (Matthew 9:27). And Jesus himself had announced that as the Messiah, on whom the Spirit of God dwelt, he would bring sight to the blind (Luke 4:18). It wasn't by accident, therefore, that they clamoured for Jesus' attention in a particular way, appealing to him as 'Son of David', a synonym for Messiah, King and Shepherd of Israel. Ordered by the crowd to be silent they shouted even louder, and did not care who knew it. Jesus stopped in his tracks, gave them his attention and wanted them to know he was listening – hence his request that they specified what they wanted. In faith, they settled for nothing less than their one concern – sight. They were not disappointed. Their burden was lifted, a new world was opened up to them, the darkness was gone and Messiah whom they now could see had done it.

Luke 19:1-10 – *Jesus and Zacchaeus*

The newer city of Jericho was a trading centre, and head of the tax collectors there was a wealthy Jew named Zacchaeus. Jesus had been popular with tax collectors and word had probably reached him through his colleagues that Jesus was worth seeing. His interest was aroused but Jesus was pressed in by the moving crowd. However the strength of his curiosity and the presence of a wide open tree with low branches along the route offset the disadvantage he had of being short. He would play it safe. He just wanted to see which one was Jesus.

In due course Jesus got to the sycamore fig tree and addressed Zacchaeus personally. He wanted Zacchaeus to take him to his house. This caused a wave of muffled protest that grew more audible both amongst the pilgrims from Galilee and the citizens of Jericho. Jesus had invited himself to be a guest of a man whose taxation activities had affected most of the local population. But Zacchaeus made the most of his opportunity. He welcomed Jesus gladly. But there was a significant development. Aware of the public feeling of resentment and of the openness on Jesus' part his conscience became active. He announced he would, there and then, restore to the rightful owners any of his ill-gotten gains, and promised to be generous to the poor. He would do as the Jewish Law demanded (Exodus 22:1; Numbers 5:6). Witnessing the evidence of this repentance, Jesus assured him that salvation had come to his house. This tax collector was a spiritual son of Abraham. And he took the opportunity to tell the crowd that the Son of Man had come to seek and to save the lost.

God's rule constitutes a test
Luke 19:11-27 – *the parable of the pounds*

Contrary to public expectation, the kingdom of God as the final worldwide event was not going to happen immediately. Instead, according to this parable, there would be a period of probation before the king's public installation in which servants of the kingdom were expected to put the king's investment to profitable use. Ten servants were therefore entrusted with a pound. How would they act? The absence of the king designate constituted an additional test for them, which was failed immediately by those who never wanted him as king in the first place, and who dispatched a delegation to tell him so. He returned however in due course as king and proceeded to oversee the day of reckoning.

Three groups were described: there were faithful servants who had used the investment wisely and who were rewarded accordingly with positions of responsibility and authority; there was a servant who did nothing because he distrusted his master as one whom he considered impossible to please and who therefore had to live with the shame of deprivation; and there were enemies whose rebellion against his appointment as king resulted in their own destruction.

Such was the clear teaching about the kingdom of God. Having been announced by John the Baptist, the theme was expounded by Jesus in detail so that there should have been no confusion in anyone's mind on the issue.

And it was at such a juncture that Jesus and his disciples arrived at the city of Jerusalem. Humanly speaking this appeared to be the final showdown involving much controversy; but from God's perspective it was to be a mission accomplished.

CHAPTER 8

Ministry at Jerusalem

Matthew 21–25, Mark 11–13, Luke 19:28 – 21

It was about 17 miles from Jericho to Jerusalem. Jesus had tried to convey several times to his followers that this visit to Jerusalem would be his last. The controversies that had arisen earlier in his ministry were now coming to a head. The disputes that would develop in Jerusalem were very intense and took place in a very short period of time, a week in fact. Some folk, admittedly, were still euphoric about their understanding of the coming of the kingdom, but Jesus knew the reality of the situation and also what his priorities were.

Fatal controversy with the Jewish leaders

Matthew 21:1–23:39, Mark 11:1–12:44, Luke 19:28–21:4

Entering Jerusalem

Matthew 21:1-11, Mark 11:1-11, Luke 19:28-44, John 12:12-19

They approached Jerusalem through the settlements of Bethphage and Bethany at the foot of the Mount of Olives. Jesus had friends there. A donkey and her colt, tied to a house door, were perfect for the next move. The colt had never been ridden. The two disciples sent to fetch them caused a query which Jesus had expected. But there was no problem. Both Matthew and John called their readers' attention to the significance of this action. In the prophecies of Isaiah (Isaiah 62:11) and Zechariah (Zechariah 9:9) it was stated that the city of Zion was to welcome her king who was a humble Messiah as indicated by the mode of transport chosen, namely a colt, the foal of a donkey.

At first, the crowd consisted of those on their way to Jerusalem. But they were joined by another crowd of people who were already at the city and who had heard that the one who had raised Lazarus to life was coming there. Cloaks were thrown on the animal, and spread on the road along with palm branches readily available from the fields. Soon the atmosphere was filled with excited shouts of triumph, peace, glory and praise that welcomed the king coming in the name of the Lord who in popular expectation would restore the kingdom of David. The Pharisees, however, felt threatened by the sight of Jesus' undiminished, even growing, popularity. Some of them asked Jesus to appeal for quiet. But that was like trying to cap a volcano! This was a singular and extraordinary day and not one for detached observation let alone critical complaint. If the crowd was silenced, the stones would start a spontaneous uproar.

Later that day, Jesus lamented the fact that the Jerusalem leadership was spiritually blind to this. Overlooking the city, he wept over it. He knew that peace and salvation would only come to them if they recognised his arrival there as God's moment of salvation. But they did not. They did not want a Messiah who was humble, merciful and just. And he knew they would have to live and die with the consequences of their choice. The city would eventually be sieged and destroyed. Briefly that evening, he noted the uproar his visit had caused, looked around the temple and then retired to Bethany. People were still talking about the prophet from Galilee.

The disturbance in the temple
Matthew 21:12-17, Mark 11:15-19, Luke 19:45-46

The next day Jesus returned to the Temple where he fuelled his enemies' animosity in at least three ways.

First, the chief priests and teachers of the law heard him when he quoted the Scripture that God had meant his temple to be a house of prayer for the people of all nations (Isaiah 56:7). Seeing the business activities of the merchants and moneychangers, Jesus used Jeremiah's words to describe it as a hideout for thieves (Jeremiah 7:11) before causing a major disturbance by overturning tables and prohibiting entry.

Then he made the leaders angrier when he followed this with miracles of mercy and power, restoring people's sight and healing people's limbs.

The last straw for them seems to have been the noise made by the children who were now shouting in the Temple what they had heard the crowds chanting the previous day – 'Hosanna to the Son of David!' Jesus defended the children by another reference to scripture (Psalm 8:2) that God perfected the praise of children and infants, and approved it. As usual, the ordinary folk loved the line Jesus took, and were amazed. But the religious leaders were now committed to killing him. They could not cope with him. They were actually afraid of him.

The episode of the fig tree
Matthew 21:17-22, Mark 11:12-14,19-25

In Mark's account, the incident involving the fig tree took place over two days, before and after Jesus' activity in the temple. It was as if in Mark's mind what happened to the fig tree was typical of what would happen to the temple and the Jewish establishment.

From a distance Jesus saw the tree's leaves. But close up, there were no figs. True, the main fig crop was later in the year, in early autumn, but early figs started in spring and though smaller were still edible. If there were leaves there should have been early figs, and any fig tree that was going to bear the main crop would have had some early figs on it. When Jesus verbally condemned the fig tree to fruitlessness, it was a fitting parable of the religious world he had just encountered. The next day, as Peter noticed, the tree was dead.

Jesus used the moment to emphasise that his disciples should have faith in God, not that the fig tree would somehow be revitalised or spared, but faith that every obstacle to God's plan would be removed. Of course, such faith could only be expressed in prayer, and any prayer was valid only if it came from a person who practised forgiveness. This was the difference between what Jesus stood for and what Judaism had become.

Jesus' authority questioned
Matthew 21:18-27, Mark 11:27-33, Luke 19:47–20:8

Jesus continued to teach the appreciative crowd in the Temple. The religious leaders still wanted him dead, but didn't want to be too obvious about it. So they had a question for him. The more he said the more chance they thought they had of catching him out. Probably with the cleansing of the temple in mind, they queried what right he had to speak and act in the way he did. Jesus made his answer to their question dependent on their answer to his. He wanted to talk about John the Baptist. John had proclaimed the coming of Messiah and baptized all who repented. Jesus wanted to know from where, in their judgement, John got his authority to baptize. Was it of God or just man's idea? This cornered them. Their fear of the public prevented them from saying it was from man, and their fear of Jesus prevented them from conceding it was from God. At the very least, the public considered Jesus to be in the same prophetic tradition as John. So they wouldn't answer. Neither then would Jesus. They would try some other ploy, but first of all Jesus told them a parable to define the issues.

The parable of the two sons
Matthew 21:28-32

A father told his two sons to go and work in the vineyard. One replied verbally and courteously that he would go, but didn't. The other who at first refused later changed his mind and went. There were just two groups – the disobedient as opposed to the repentant. The words that were spoken were simply irrelevant. Whatever he might have said to the contrary, one son remained the embodiment of disobedience, the other of repentance. The application was obvious. Tax collectors and prostitutes listened believingly to John the Baptist and repented; but the Jewish leaders in unbelief would not travel the righteous path

John had proclaimed. It was clear who would enter the kingdom of God. Here was another call to believe and repent. Jesus followed it with another parable.

The parable of the tenants of the vineyard
Matthew 21:33-46, Mark 12:1-12, Luke 20:9-20

The plain fact was that the Jewish leaders, both past and present, had abused the whole concept of the kingdom of God. God, like a responsible landowner who planted a vineyard and let it out to tenants, had set up a covenant people and entrusted its management to human leaders. The whole point of a vineyard was to produce fruit. But the tenants wanted full control, and defended their selfish interests by seeing off all the representatives the owner sent to receive the harvest. When God over many decades had sent prophets to Israel looking for spiritual fruit, they had been consistently shamed and even killed by the political and priestly powers. The latest victim had been John the Baptist. Jesus, pictured in the parable as the owner's son, would share the same fate.

The parable was aimed at the teachers of the Law, the Pharisees and the chief priests, and they knew it, for they had made their minds up to arrest Jesus. But before they disappeared to do their evil deeds, they needed to be reminded of the outcome. They would be destroyed, and the kingdom, entrusted to other tenants, would survive under the stewardship of a different race. God would have a new people who would produce the desired fruit.

This was unthinkable to many of his listeners, but Jesus quoted another scripture to clinch his point (Psalm 118:22). This concerned a stone which had been prepared as a crucial stone with a crucial function but which the builders had rejected as worthless. Despite the Sanhedrin's rejection of their one true Messiah, God would exalt his Anointed One and give him his rightful place. And the new race, which would be identified as spiritual Israel, comprising Jew and Gentile, would refer to this psalm more than once. Peter quoted it in his defence to the Sanhedrin (Acts 4:11) and commented about it quite profoundly in his first letter (1 Peter 2:4-9).

Developing the story, Jesus made another point. If the stone was not incorporated into the building where it belonged, it would lie around as a hazard for people to fall over. And Jesus was indeed a stumbling stone to the leaders of his day. Furthermore, in a possible allusion to Daniel's vision (Daniel 2), he warned that should that stone fall on anyone it would crush that person to dust.

Things were being said now that meant the confrontation would get more serious. And Jesus wasn't about to back off. He had more to say to the public about the kingdom of God and people's attitude to it.

The parable of the prince's wedding feast
Matthew 22:1-14

Jesus thought it appropriate to speak of the kingdom of God in terms of a banquet, even a royal banquet for the wedding of the king's son. The prophets had given the Jewish nation ample notice of the kingdom of God in the same way that the wedding invitations in the story had gone out in good time. But it was when the customary reminders were sent nearer to the event that a problem emerged. A bad initial response was followed by an even worse one. Some of the invited guests simply couldn't be bothered about it, having more pressing things to do, but others were violent and murderous to the messengers.

The king's response was to exclude and punish those who had been invited, and to open up the feast to a completely different group. This was a repetition of the point made by other parables that the Jewish rejection of the kingdom would be followed by the inclusion of the Gentiles. All wedding guests, however, whoever they were, were expected to wear the wedding garment which it would seem was given to each guest on entry. It was the official sign of a recognised guest. All who were without it were gate crashers who didn't stay in for long. The meaning of this wedding garment has to be understood in the context of Jesus' dispute with the Jewish leaders, in which case I think that the identifying mark Jesus was referring to was John's baptism of repentance.

The issue of taxes paid to Rome
Matthew 22:15-22, Mark 12:13-17, Luke 20:20-26

But the Pharisees had just one thing on their mind now: how to hand Jesus over to the legislative power of the Roman Governor. Their plan was to get him involved in political issues, so they bribed some men to approach him with sweet talk before innocently enquiring how his interpretation of the Jewish law viewed the payment of taxes to Rome. Jesus didn't fall for the flattery and he also steered clear of any mention of the law. He knew that any hint of refusal to pay tax would be construed as politically subversive. So instead, he addressed the questioners as hypocrites; and when handed the coin that was used for the tax, focussed on the Emperor's name and image. It was obviously a Roman coin. So pay Rome what belongs to Rome, and pay God what belongs to God. Brilliant!

The Sadducees and the resurrection
Matthew 22:23-33, Mark 12:18-27, Luke 20:27-39

Some Sadducees also had a question that was related to the Law. They did not believe in the resurrection or life after death, and so for their amusement presented a scenario to Jesus which they had probably used before. A woman in her lifetime had in turn been the wife of seven brothers. Who would be her husband in the resurrection? Jesus observed that they were reduced to asking such silly questions because of their rationalistic approach to the Scriptures and God's power. But he would answer it nevertheless. Marriage was instituted for human society on earth. In the resurrection mode of life there was therefore no need for it. There was no possibility of death there either. Scripture portrayed the living God as the God only of the living. Jesus illustrated his point with reference to Abraham, Isaac and Jacob. After they had died, God told Moses that he was still their God – which would not have been the case if they had not lived on. Physical death did not have the last word. That always belonged to God. And God had said, 'I *am* the God of Abraham, the God of

Isaac, and the God of Jacob' (Matthew 22:32, italics mine). Among the amazed crowds, even some teachers of the law thought Jesus had handled the question well.

The greatest of the commandments
Matthew 22:34-40, Mark 12:28-34

One of the teachers of the Law had a follow up question about which was the most important commandment in the law. He himself may have been sincere, but at least he was being used by the group of Pharisees who were still attempting to ensnare Jesus into indiscreet comments. Jesus was clear. The first and most important one was that Israel love the Lord her God with all the heart, soul, mind, and strength. He was the only God. The corollary of that was the law's requirement to love one's neighbour as oneself. These were foundational. The teacher of the Law agreed, saying that obedience to them was more important than animal sacrifices. Whether he meant to embroil Jesus in a discussion about the Jewish sacrificial system is not clear. Jesus certainly recognised the truth of his answer but did not pursue the comparison. He simply said that the man was not far from the kingdom of God.

Jesus' question concerning the Messiah
Matthew 22:41-46, Mark 12:35-37, Luke 20:41-44

Before the group of Pharisees had the chance to set a further agenda, Jesus set them a question: What did they think about the Messiah? Whose descendant was he? How did the designation 'David's descendant' square with the fact that, in Psalm 110:1, the Holy Spirit inspired the same David to refer to him as 'my Lord?' There was no answer, but there didn't need to be. Jesus' point was that Jewish thinking about the 'Son of David' could so easily hide the more important truth that Messiah had a status greater than any claim based on heredity. It was a status conferred directly on him by Yahweh.

Jesus' warning about the Pharisees and teachers of the law Matthew 23:1-39, Mark 12:38-44, Luke 20:45–21:4

Making use of a lull in the questions, Jesus took the chance to warn his largely sympathetic audience that they should defend themselves against the teachers of the Law. The problem was that their exploitative and ambitious behaviour was inconsistent with their role as the authorised interpreters of Moses' law.

It was very clear what Jesus thought about them. He had a list of complaints which all sprang from the fact that they had no conception of what it was to be a servant. They wanted to be the centre of attention. They made burdensome pronouncements for the people but offered no support and had no conscience about depriving widows of their homes. Long public prayers and scripture verses worn on the forehead and arms were done just to make an impression. They basked in the special treatment given them at feasts and at the synagogue. They liked the dignity of the long robe and the verbal respect of being addressed as Teacher. This, Jesus said, was completely out of place in his kingdom. No human should be elevated to the status of 'Teacher', 'Father' or 'Leader'. Messiah was the Leader, there was one Father (in heaven) and their one teacher was Jesus who when he left would be replaced by the Holy Spirit.

The Pharisees and the teachers of the law would be judged as hypocrites. They were a hindrance to people who wished to enter the kingdom of heaven, and put all their efforts into their own program of proselytising which would end up in hell. They had pernickety rules about tithing and oaths made by the Temple and the altar, but had no knowledge of the living God and had no interest in justice, mercy and honesty. They were like whitewashed tombs. Their outward appearance disguised their selfishness, violence and hypocrisy. Theirs was a religion of death. They were snakes and belonged in hell.

In striking contrast to the Pharisees was a poor widow who was the victim of the system which the ostentatious and overbearing Pharisees had set up. Jesus used her as an object lesson as he sat near the Temple treasury and saw what the people gave. He knew what sacrifice her gift of two small copper coins meant, for after meeting her obligations she had nothing left to live on. This was an example of unforgivable exploitation of the poor that justified his quite blistering attack on the Jewish leadership. Jesus would understand, sympathise with and deliver folk from a whole range of human imperfections, but the one thing he could not stomach was hypocrisy.

Jerusalem's refusal of Jesus' way would spell their fate, meaning that the temple would be abandoned.

Preparing for the future – the Olivet discourse
Matthew 24-25, Mark 13, Luke 21

What the disciples should expect
Matthew 24:1-28, Mark 13:1-23, Luke 21:5-24

It was time to leave the temple. Before he did so, Jesus heard admiring comments by folk who were impressed by its architectural features and religious purpose. It was indeed an imposing structure. But Jesus commented that it would not last. He spoke deliberately and was emphatic. Those stones would one day be nothing more than a heap of rubble.

When they reached the Mount of Olives, Peter, James, John and Andrew asked Jesus for some clarification. They wanted to know when the catastrophe would happen and what the warning sign would be. According to Matthew's record, they seem to have thought that the destruction of the temple would coincide with Jesus' return and the end of the age.

But they were mistaken. So Jesus took pains to separate the three ideas – on one hand all the events relating to the temple would happen within the life span of that generation; but then he made statements like 'the end is not yet', and 'don't be deceived by anyone who says the time is near.' The three things were not going to take place at the same time. He needed to give them a guide as to how things would develop, and so we have his outline summary of the sorts of things they could expect, starting with the destruction of the temple right up to his second coming.

He was concerned above all else to eliminate the twin dangers of *deception* and *alarm*: first, they were to be alert enough not to be taken in by messianic impostors whose claims he knew would be persuasive enough to gain a following; and then, they were to ensure they maintained their balance and stayed calm even when world events may suggest otherwise. Yes there would be military confrontations, political and social revolutions, nationalist unrest, famines, earthquakes, and even signs in space. But these were not the signs of the end of the world. They should rather be viewed, like labour pains, as the beginning of a new era. The completion of a pregnancy involved upheaval, but it was an upheaval that led to the joy of welcoming a new life. Jesus' emphasis was pastoral. Joy would replace trouble. When witnessing these traumatic events, Jesus' followers were to live in the expectation that something new was about to arrive.

Of more contemporary and continuing relevance was the *persecution* that Jesus' disciples would suffer throughout the period at the hands of both the religious and civic authorities. It would happen solely because of their loyalty to him. Some would experience physical torture, imprisonment without trial and even state sponsored murder. All would be hated. And such hatred would not be confined to the Roman or Jewish councils. All nations would be involved. Of course, the prospect of persecution would sift the real disciples from the apparent ones. Many would repudiate and abandon the faith in what would be nothing less than a *great apostasy.* At least two disconcerting features were linked to this. First, Jesus' followers could expect to be betrayed by any one of their immediate family members or close friends, whether parent, child or sibling. Secondly, false prophets would appear so that folk who were already facing upheaval would hear conflicting messages. In the face of such intense wickedness and general coldness of heart Jesus saw the need to warn all of his followers to be on their guard and stand firm for him.

For it was not all gloom. The other side of the coin was that such persecution would serve to confirm their faith and spread the gospel. In the first place, it was by standing firm to the end that they would survive, gain life and salvation. But also, Jesus promised that when in their commitment to him his followers made their defence, the Holy Spirit would take over. There was no need for them to worry beforehand over what to say; they just had to speak the truth that was relevant at the time. They were to expect to be given wisdom at the appropriate moment so that they would become convincing witnesses even to governors and kings. In this way the gospel of the kingdom of God would reach all nations. And, incidentally, it was when the whole world was reached, that the end would come.

Jesus very practically put the emphasis on gospel preaching, thus lifting the whole issue from the realm of the abstract and speculative. He had given them enough information for them to put into practice. His followers were not to be deceived by the false prophets, alarmed by world events or deflected by apostasy or persecution.

After this synopsis, Jesus returned to the then current situation about the destruction of Jerusalem, an event which would introduce a time of great distress (Matthew 24:15-28, Mark 13:14-23, Luke 21:20-24). Using a phrase from the book of Daniel, he spoke about 'the abomination that causes desolation.' It would stand in the holy place where it did not belong. He was referring to the military aggression of idolatrous Rome. The sight of Rome's armies surrounding Jerusalem would spell the city's pending desolation. Luke added the solemn explanation that this was the time of punishment fulfilling what had been written. The city of Jerusalem would afford no protection at all for the inhabitants of Judaea. So the disciples were to head for the hills in the clothes they were wearing. Armies did not show any consideration even for pregnant women and nursing mothers. Jerusalem would be devastated under Gentile tyranny, just as Jesus had said: 'Your house is left to you desolate.' It would be a period of unparalleled distress, death and displacement as Gentile domination of the city would continue seemingly unchecked.

But again, Jesus deliberately distinguished this disaster from the event of his coming. He said that rumours would abound that the Messiah had returned. But they would not be true. Therefore it would simply be a waste of time and energy to listen to anyone who claimed they had located the Messiah in some secret room or desert place, whatever signs and miracles they used to back up their report. Lies and deceit belonged, like a carcass, to the realm of death around which vultures gathered. The simple fact was that Jesus would not be returning when Jerusalem was destroyed. When he did return there would be no scope for any doubt or uncertainty – it would, like the sheet lightning, be plain for all to see.

The return of Jesus in glory
Matthew 24:29-31, Mark 13:24-27, Luke 21:25-28

Jesus then addressed the theme of the end of the age and his return. This was the goal of history. It would occur after the great distress he had just mentioned. In some way, the people of God would be given considerate treatment. Those days of grief and woe would be 'cut short' for their sake, meaning that they would survive the hardship to welcome the return of their Lord. His coming would be introduced by signs in the sun, moon, stars and planets, and irregularities in the sea. Whereas mankind in general would be in a state of apprehension, the disciples of Jesus were encouraged to expect redemption. They would not be disappointed – the sign of the Son of Man would be seen in the sky as Jesus arrived in glory, power and authority. Angels would attend him, and with a loud trumpet call he would gather his people wherever they may be. These details would be incorporated into Paul's more detailed words in 1 Thessalonians 4:16-17.

The parable of the fig tree
Matthew 24:32-35, Mark 13:28-31, Luke 21:29-33

Having shed light on the three issues of the destruction of the temple, his return and the end of the age, Jesus returned to his contemporary situation and spoke of things that his own generation would witness. There was a lesson to learn from the fig tree. In the same way that the sight of its tender twigs and fresh leaves heralded summer, trials such as the persecution of Christians and the abomination that caused desolation would certainly herald the coming judgement of Jerusalem and the vindication of the kingdom of God. The book of Acts records the growth and spread of that kingdom, as the old order was replaced by the new. The temple and city would be gone soon, but Jesus' words would never become obsolete.

The call to be prepared
Matthew 24:36–25:46, Mark 13:32-37, Luke 21:34-36

Jesus proceeded to apply the truth about his coming. Its date was unknown, and it was futile to guess. Because this was so, life would continue as normal until the critical moment when it would be too late for any preparation. It wasn't enough, said Jesus, simply to know in advance that he would come again. Noah had warned folk about the coming flood, but those who did not act upon that knowledge in making the required arrangements well in advance were overtaken by the judgement. This would be the case at his coming. The unprepared person would be taken away in judgement while another who had acted on the information would be spared. There would be those whose lifestyles remained a continual indulgence in gluttony and drink, and who would therefore be preoccupied with the sickness and hangovers that were the result. Others would be equally preoccupied with life's worries. For such people, he warned, his coming would be an unexpected shock, like a mousetrap to the mouse, or a burglar to the household. This was a universal warning. But there was a way to overcome the threat of such 'burglary' – stay awake, stay alert, and maintain the attitude of prayer.

Jesus then gave four parables to explain how his followers could make the necessary adequate preparations for his coming.

The parable of the house servant: Matthew 24:45-51

'Staying alert' meant *serving*. If the coming of Jesus was delayed (as it has turned out to be) and unexpected (as it still is), the way to live in a state of readiness for it was simply to be faithful to the tasks he had given his people to do. His people were in this for the long haul. And Jesus expected them to serve. Like a servant put in charge, they were to maintain their obedience and show dependable faithfulness. They were to avoid complacent presumption, self-indulgence and abuse of others and make sure other's needs were met.

The parable of the bridesmaids: Matthew 25:1-13

'Staying alert' involved *habitual self-examination.* Jesus said that this parable would become more relevant as time went by. It teaches the wisdom of self-assessment that was necessary in maintaining the state of readiness. The ten girls who were preparing the bride to meet the bridegroom would be expecting the groom to come to the bride's house. Everyone in the subsequent procession to the groom's house was required to carry his or her own lamp – but lamps use up oil. All the girls had enough oil at the beginning to light their lamps. But the wise girls ensured that their lamps could be replenished by their reserve flask of oil. To be ready meant checking regularly how much oil was left. A sudden shout was the only warning of the bridegroom's arrival. And a depleted oil supply at that moment meant that five girls were looking for the shops instead of getting to the feast at the bridegroom's house.

The parable of the talents: Matthew 25:14-30

'Staying alert' meant recognising and honouring the concept of *stewardship.* God entrusted to each one an investment commensurate with the person's ability. Whatever the amount, all were to put his gifts to use in order to increase the yield. Wisdom lay in the taking of positive and responsible initiatives. The good and faithful servants took into account the fact that they had enough time to put the assigned funds to work. They actively planned for the future and were invited to share in the master's celebration. The lazy man returned the gift and incurred his master's wrath.

The parable of the sheep and goats: Matthew 25:31-46

'Staying alert' meant living a righteous life in terms of *compassion.* This was how the spirit of salvation was actually lived out. Two groups dispersed throughout all nations were 'the righteous' and the others. True righteousness was evidenced by compassion, a goal that was achieved by God's love and grace. When Messiah's disciples supported the weakest of Jesus' followers, Jesus took it as done for him – whether as refugees they were deprived of food, water, clothes or home, or as victimised disciples had been unjustly imprisoned. These 'sheep', blessed by the king's Father, discovered that the kingdom had been eternally prepared for them; their service on earth was done as unto the Lord and they were welcomed to take their inheritance, eternal life. The goats by contrast departed to the place prepared for the devil; they had displayed no evidence of righteousness.

Immediately after this teaching as to how to live in the light of his coming, Jesus turned his thoughts to his approaching death. He as the Son of Man was to suffer death by crucifixion. What he had said must happen was about to happen.

CHAPTER 9

Mission Accomplished

Matthew 26–28, Mark 14–16, Luke 22–24, John 12–21

Jesus had tried to make it clear to his disciples that his death and resurrection were two imperatives. There could be no kingdom on any other basis. He used the word 'must' – not only in the synoptic gospels but also in John's gospel.

To Nicodemus (John 3), he had said that sight of and entry to the kingdom of God was dependent upon a change so radical it could only be described as a new birth, or a birth from above. This new life, said Jesus, could be achieved only by the Holy Spirit, the agent of life. But Jesus then continued – equally imperative in the matter of having eternal life was the fact that the Son of Man, the Messiah, was to be 'lifted up' as the focal point of faith. By these words Jesus had meant his death by crucifixion. That time had now come. Jesus knew that if the kingdom of God was to become a spiritual force in his followers' lives then his death was necessary. It would be the only solid basis for the forgiveness of sins.

Messiah's arrest and trial

Matthew 26:1–27:26, Mark 14:1–15:15, Luke 22:1–23:25, John 12:2-8, 13:1-30, 18:1–19:16

Enemies and friends

Matthew 26:1-16, Mark 14:1-11, Luke 22:1-6

The Passover meal was part of the Feast of Unleavened Bread. The crowds that thronged Jerusalem for this could well have posed a problem to the enemies of Jesus who were adamantly committed to destroying him. They wanted to avoid any hint of a riot which would have caused all sorts of serious political complications. So in the residence of Caiaphas the high priest, the priests, elders and the teachers of the law got their heads together to formulate a strategy. The task surely couldn't be insurmountable, not if it was done subtly.

Meanwhile at Bethany Jesus was relaxing with friends all of whom had good reasons to be grateful to him. The venue was the home of a man, Simon, whom Jesus had possibly healed of leprosy. This was to be Mary's moment. She had a precious alabaster jar of quality perfume, worth a year's wages. As Jesus reclined at the meal in the way they did then, she anointed Jesus' head and feet emptying the lot, a pint of pure nard. Her hair became the towel. The fragrance was not just on Jesus and on her but also wafted through the home. But her action divided opinion. A discordant note interrupted the pleasant atmosphere. The spokesman for a number of Jesus' disciples was Judas. What a waste! Where was her social conscience? As they stood in harsh judgment over Mary, John inserted a rather ominous note about Judas and his love of money. It was about to feature very strongly. If Judas would sell his master because of his love of silver, Mary would sacrifice her stuff for love of Jesus. In Jesus' opinion Mary's deed was refreshingly beautiful. It would adorn the gospel wherever it was preached.

But that was the last thing on Judas' mind. Controlled by Satan, the adversary (Luke 22:3), he left the fragrant room at Bethany for the enemy's headquarters to make a deal with the chief priests and the temple guard. Treachery carried its reward. So he would put Jesus in their power for thirty pieces of silver. He would pick the right moment which wouldn't cause a riot. They were delighted.

The Passover meal
Matthew 26:17-29, Mark 14:12-25, Luke 22:7-30, John 13:1-30

The Passover was the annual Jewish festival followed by the week-long festival of Unleavened Bread. They were so closely associated that the term Passover applied to both. The festival commemorated God's deliverance of the Hebrews from their slavery in Egypt when, secure in their houses marked by the blood of the Passover lamb, the people ate a hasty meal as God brought judgment on Egypt's firstborn. Unleavened bread would be their diet for the first days of their wilderness journey. Over time, what was known as the Egyptian Hallel (Psalms 113 to 118) was sung at the meal. This was interesting, because it was Psalm 118 that included two statements relevant to Jesus: 'Blessed is he that comes in the name of the Lord', and 'The stone that the builders rejected has become the head of the corner.'

Jesus had all the arrangements in hand. Peter and John would be met by a man with a jar of water who would lead them to a specific house where a large upper room had been prepared as a guest room. The group arrived at evening and when the meal had got under way, Jesus told them what he knew. One of them was a traitor. Yes, it was necessary for him to fulfil the scriptural prophecy, but that was no excuse for betrayal and did not cancel out human accountability. Judas murmured some mild protest probably for the benefit of the others present. But he knew that Jesus knew what he was up to. Jesus told him so.

Notwithstanding the sadness and tension of the situation, Jesus proceeded to give his disciples some important truths. For him, this Passover was the last of its kind as the whole thing was to find a new fulfilment in the kingdom of God. He seems to have been referring to the time after the day of Pentecost when he would enjoy spiritual fellowship with his followers in the newly constituted church community. The bread they were eating was a symbol of his body given for them. The cup of wine was a symbol of his blood as the seal of the promised new covenant, through which forgiveness of sins could be enjoyed by his people. But whether they grasped any of this at that time is very doubtful. They were still wondering who the betrayer was and actually started a debate as to who among the group was the greatest. Incredible!

Jesus had to step in to break up the argument. He reminded them that in the kingdom the notion of authority was related to that of the servant spirit. He had been their role model and mentor in this all the time he had led them. (This is emphasised by John in his record of Jesus washing the disciples' feet.) And this would not change after he had ascended. As his apostles, they were to maintain their own fellowship with him at the table of remembrance and mediate his authority to the church. Again, they didn't get the message. Even after the resurrection they would still be entertaining ideas of an earthly kingdom based in Jerusalem – whereas in Jesus' list of priorities, top of the list was the coming of the Holy Spirit to give them power to be his witnesses throughout the whole world (Acts 1:8).

They sang the Passover hymn and Judas left the room. After the teaching that is recorded in John 14, the rest of the party left the house.

Prayerfully fulfilling the Father's plan
Matthew 26:30-56, Mark 14:26-52, Luke 22:31-53, John 18:2-12

Jesus was acutely conscious that things were about to change. He knew it on the basis of two Old Testament statements he said were about to be fulfilled. First, Zechariah 13:7 had spoken of the shepherd being stricken and the flock being scattered; secondly, Isaiah 53:12 had described the servant of Yahweh as being numbered with the transgressors.

He thus announced to his little flock that they would all without exception fall away, but that after his resurrection he would meet up with them in Galilee. True to form, they all objected, particularly Peter. Fall away? Never! They would stay firm till the moment of death. They did not know that Satan had already targeted Peter and that Jesus had already prayed for him. Fall he would, but in faith would be restored.

Speaking figuratively, he told them to sell their cloaks and buy a sword. There had been a time when they had been provided for and welcomed by the public. But those days had passed and had given way to a time when they would need to fend for themselves. They took his words literally, however, and produced two swords, so Jesus gave up trying to get through to them.

He felt the need to pray. And when they all reached the garden at Gethsemane he told the eleven to do the same, otherwise they would surely crumble before the oncoming temptation. Eight of them sat in a far from happy group. Sleep came easily to them. Jesus went a short distance away and took Peter, James and John for support. He told them he was deeply distressed and troubled and asked them to stay on watch, physically and spiritually. Flat on his face in three sessions of prayer he poured his heart out to the Father. He wished the hour would pass and the cup taken away from him. But if he had to drink it, he would bow to the Father's will. His anguish of heart heightened the intensity as the sweat falling off him became like droplets of blood. But angelic support strengthened him. Meanwhile the two groups of disciples, oblivious to his spiritual struggle, had given in to their heavy hearts and heavy eyelids. They were awakened by the voice of Jesus telling them that the moment of betrayal was upon them.

Judas had known when and where to come. He was with some Roman soldiers and followed by a large crowd in the pay of the Jewish leaders who carried lanterns, torches, swords and clubs. Prepared for the worst, Jesus maintained his dignity throughout the whole dirty business. He established who it was they were looking for and promptly made himself known so that his disciples could go. His enemies fell backwards at his announcement as he had used the name of Yahweh, 'I am.' There was therefore now no need for Judas to have identified Jesus but he proceeded anyway with the arranged signal as confirmation. At this kiss of betrayal, Jesus was physically seized and arrested. Simon Peter sprang into action and used his sword with drastic results for Malchus, a servant of the high priest.

To Judas, Jesus showed civility, even calling him 'Friend.' To Peter, Jesus issued a rebuke. No swords. All who lived that way would die that way. If he needed any defence he would get angelic assistance by prayer to his Father. But the Father's will was that he drank the cup he was given. Reaching out to Malchus, Jesus touched his ear and healed him. To the crowd, Jesus asked why they needed those weapons. He was a teacher not a political agitator. But spiritual darkness reigned. Suddenly, all the disciples were gone, and Jesus left as a lamb for the slaughter. The last to go was a young man who had been secretly observing everything. He was forced to slip out of all his clothes and run home naked. This could well have been Mark.

At the palace of the high priests, Annas and Caiaphas
Matthew 26:57-75, 27:3-10, Mark 14:53-72, Luke 22:54-71, John 18:12-27

The Roman soldiers took the bound figure of Jesus to Annas, the head of the priestly party in Jerusalem which owed its status to the will of the Roman governor. Annas had once been high priest, and as the father of five high priests and father-in-law of the current one still retained a tremendous amount of influence. When he interrogated Jesus about his followers and teaching, he got nowhere. Jesus pointed out that his teaching had been public enough, and the high priest should question his hearers. He got slapped by one of the guards as if he had been disrespectful.

The next place was the house of Caiaphas the high priest where an official hearing took place. The entire Jewish leadership was present. Witnesses gave garbled and inaccurate versions of the occasion when Jesus had spoken about his bodily resurrection in terms of 'rebuilding this temple in three days.' He had, however, never said he would destroy anything! Before all this false testimony he stayed silent. Caiaphas knew that no successful accusation would emerge from such inconsistent statements. But self-incrimination was possible. So Caiaphas illegally put Jesus on oath to answer the charge that he had claimed to be the Messiah and the Son of God. At this Jesus broke his silence. He would not hide that fact, and actually affirmed that he as the Son of Man would sit at the right hand of God and come again on the clouds of heaven. Now if that was a false claim, as to them it surely must have been, it was blasphemy. They now had the line they could follow and if they unanimously agreed he was worthy of death all they had to do was twist the Roman governor's arm. Confident of their success now, they treated Jesus as already condemned. They spat in his face, blindfolded him, struck him with their fists and then mockingly invited him to prophesy who had done it. It never entered the heads of any one on that Council what the repercussions would be if they were wrong!

During the couple of hours or so that Jesus was being interrogated by Annas and Caiaphas, Simon Peter was enduring a different sort of personal ordeal in the courtyard of the high priest. A reading of the four different accounts gives a sense of the prolonged bombardment he was under. The girl at the gate asked him if he was a disciple of the man just brought in. He dismissed her question with a 'No'. He moved away but stayed around because he wanted to see how things would work out. But at a charcoal fire in the centre of the courtyard another servant started off a public discussion when she pointedly identified him as one who was with Jesus of Nazareth. He denied it and tried to make out he didn't understand what they were talking about. So he moved away from the fire. But the comments kept coming. Folk had noted his Galilean accent and some wondered if they had seen him in the garden. One of these was ominously a relative of Malchus. His language became stronger as he stuck to his denial with oaths and curses. A rooster crowed again and Peter's memory kicked in. He got out at last, but broke down and wept bitterly.

When Judas Iscariot saw that Jesus was to be sent to the Roman governor, he realised with deep regret what he had done. Whatever his secondary motives might have been, money had blinded him to reality. Jesus had submitted to the authorities and stood condemned. He returned the thirty silver coins and confirmed Jesus' innocence. But they simply could not have cared any less. Alone and guilt ridden Judas discarded the money in the temple and committed suicide. The chief priests, concerned to distinguish the secular from the religious, decided to use the 'blood money' to buy a potter's field as a burial place for foreigners. The Christian church later viewed this whole business as fulfilling the words of the prophets Jeremiah and Zechariah.

At the palace of the Roman governor, Pontius Pilate
Matthew 27:1-2,11-26, Mark 15:1-15, Luke 23:1-25, John 18:28–19:16

Taken from the headquarters of the Jewish religion, Jesus next had to face examination by Pontius Pilate, the Roman governor. It was very early in the morning. The Jewish leaders stayed outside, more concerned with their ritual cleansing than with damaging their souls. If no substantial accusation could be presented, Pilate would dismiss the case and refer it back to the Jews. That was a problem as they did not have the power of execution. The charge of blasphemy needed to be injected with the threat of political agitation and subversion. The accusation ultimately was that Jesus had incited the people to refuse to pay taxes to Rome and had set himself up as Messiah.

Pilate was open with Jesus and checked this out. Was he the king of the Jews? Jesus made it quite clear how Pilate should understand his answer. His kingdom was real, but it was not a worldly one. It was one that deplored violence and was committed to propagating truth. Anyone interested in truth would give him a hearing. It was why he had been born. That was all Pilate got from Jesus, and it was no reason to condemn him. But when he told this to the chief priests and the crowds they pointed out that his teaching had started riots in Judea that had begun in Galilee. They were of course lying.

The mention of Galilee gave Pilate an idea. Herod Antipas was then in Jerusalem. He might uncover something. Herod who had listened to John the Baptist and had been impressed with the reports about Jesus wanted to see him perform a miracle. But Jesus maintained his silence even though the chief priests and the teachers of the law kept up their barrage of accusations. For Herod, religion was fair game, so he and his soldiers indulged in some mockery (which included a fine robe) and returned Jesus to Pilate. This alliance between Herod and Pilate, according to Acts 4:27, was viewed by the early Christian church as a fulfilment of yet another scripture.

Pilate needed to make progress, so he tried to sum up the position to the Jewish leaders. Neither he nor Herod had found Jesus guilty of any crime. He did not deserve death. But because the Jews were so adamant, an acceptable compromise might be to whip the accused after which he would have to free him. This too was unlawful. Only condemned men were whipped prior to crucifixion. More mockery followed which involved a crown of thorns and a royal robe. Pilate would continue to protest that there was no reason to condemn Jesus, but his decision served only to heighten the crowd's demand that he follow the whipping with crucifixion. Blasphemers ought to die according to Jewish law.

Pilate's indecision was not helped by trying to consider three sources of information – the Jews, Jesus and his own wife. The Jews wanted crucifixion. Pilate knew their motive was evil and reminded Jesus privately that it was he, Pilate, who had the power of life and death. Jesus did not agree. God it was who had ultimate authority and Caiaphas it was who was guilty of a more serious sin. At some point in that judgment hall Pilate's wife sent him a message not to get involved. She had had a dream the previous night involving the innocent man and she hadn't enjoyed it.

His next move was to appeal to the crowd with the special Passover amnesty that had been introduced by the Roman governor. In custody was a criminal notorious for insurgency, riot and murder – Jesus Barabbas. Pilate would present the Jews with a choice – Jesus Barabbas or Jesus called Christ. But the chief priests and the elders were one step ahead. They controlled the crowd who chose Barabbas to be freed. As if amazed, Pilate asked what should become of the innocent Jesus Christ, but he already knew their answer. His attempts to release Jesus from custody were met with the Jewish charge that anyone who claimed to be Messiah was guilty of treason against the Emperor. The priests themselves had pledged loyalty to the Emperor and expected no less of the governor.

At around 6 a.m. Pilate had come to the end of the line. Mob rule had won. He didn't want any more trouble. Symbolically he washed his hands publicly of the whole affair. This was not his doing. He had made his case. The crowd told him they and their children would take any blame. They just wanted Jesus crucified. Pilate had verbally debated with them, but in practice he did what they wanted. Barabbas was released, but not his two accomplices.

It is pretty clear that if Jesus had wanted to he could have escaped the penalty of death. But he submitted quietly, offered no defence and knew his innocence all along. What sort of personality purposely submits to indignity, shame, mockery and torture when it could have been avoided? The answer we Christians give is that he was deliberately and consciously fulfilling the Father's agenda to take the curse of the law that we deserved. We could not have paid the penalty for our sins and stayed alive. There is no other reason for Jesus to have done what he did.

Nobody other than Jesus really understood what was happening – even though he had repeatedly told his disciples that he had to suffer and die and rise again. He had talked in terms of a cup, a baptism and a ransom. But nobody understood his words because nobody appreciated the problem. The problem was that of sin and its penalty under the law, spiritual death, satanic slavery and God's eternal justice. It is the same today.

Messiah's crucifixion

Matthew 27:27-66, Mark 15:16-47, Luke 23:26-56, John 19:17-42

Jesus abused by soldiers

Matthew 27:27-31, Mark 15:16-20

All that the Roman soldiers were interested in was self-indulgent entertainment. And anyone was fair game. They had no compunction about taunting helpless victims. The more ingenious the taunt the greater became the entertainment. Mockery is never healthy. True laughter does not indulge its wit at the expense of others. There being no crime committed, the soldiers resorted to mockery of Jesus' claims to be a king. In the courtyard of the governor's palace the soldiers gathered to enjoy the sport of scourging. A scarlet tunic was a mock imitation of the royal purple; the crown of thorns represented a mock victor's garland, a branch served as sceptre and the mock salute was based on *Ave Caesar.* The soldiers added the insults already used by the Jewish Sanhedrin who had also spat in his face and beaten him. It went on for some time. They considered it such good fun! But finally, the garments of mockery were removed. That psychological and emotional stage was over. Worse was to come.

Going to Golgotha

Matthew 27:32-34, Mark 15:21-23, Luke 23:26-32, John 19:17

The soldiers led Jesus away with two others – both convicted criminals. Part of the humiliation of crucifixion was that the victim carried his own cross, very much like someone forced to dig their own grave. But Jesus by now was showing signs of physical weakness. The previous busy day had ended with the ordeal in Gethsemane, betrayal and desertion. A sleepless night had been occupied by threatening and hostile interrogation from Annas, Caiaphas, Pilate, Herod and Pilate again. All of this plus the scourging had taken its toll.

A member of the public was travelling into the city. This was Simon, from a city in North Africa, Cyrene, whose sons are named as Alexander and Rufus. This detail points to the probability that he later became known in the Christian church (as probably did Jairus, Bartimaeus and Zacchaeus). Simon was forced into service, carrying Jesus' cross as Jesus walked in front. He would have been close enough to hear Jesus' words, in particular what he had to say to some Jerusalem women in the large procession who were weeping and wailing. They were to reserve their tears for themselves and their children during the coming catastrophe when they would wish they had never had children and when death would become a sweet option. If the innocent were being killed for no crime at all, then what atrocities would full scale rebellion incur? After all, dry wood burned better than green.

They arrived at a skull shaped hill outside Jerusalem. From the Mount of Olives, the rock-hewn tombs resembled the eyes of a skull. In Hebrew and Aramaic it is 'Golgotha', but it has come over to English through the Latin, 'Calvary'. Jesus tasted and refused to drink the drugged wine which women brought to lessen the pain. He wanted to have a clear mind.

From 9 a.m. till noon
Matthew 27:35-44, Mark 15:24-32, Luke 23:33-43, John 19:18-27

Crucifixion was a familiar picture under Roman rule. Jesus was nailed, hands and feet, to the cross before it was raised. It was not so high, but it would drop with a body shaking jar into its socket. The crime committed was usually hung on a placard around the neck of the victim on the way to execution and then fixed to his cross. In Jesus' case Pilate had written in Hebrew, Latin, and Greek: 'This is Jesus of Nazareth, the King of the Jews.' The chief priests took issue with this, and wanted it changed to express the crime of blasphemy. But Pilate dismissed them. He had had enough by then.

It was now 9 a.m. Jesus prayed for forgiveness for the Roman soldiers who were dutifully carrying out the orders of their superiors. The two violent robbers, probably members of the band of Barabbas on whose cross Jesus now hung, were crucified on each side of him. The soldiers threw their dice, the prize being his garments which John saw as a fulfilment of Psalm 22. Then all they could do was watch him slowly weaken and die.

The Jews now took their turn to mock Jesus. To them the predicament he was in proved that he had made hasty, extravagant and empty claims which he could not justify. Passers-by and bystanders shook their heads in judgemental disbelief. So he was the one who would tear down the Temple and build it back up in three days! He looked as if he needed to save himself! They were quoting the words of the false witnesses at his hearing and misquoting him. But Jesus was in no condition to engage in any debate. They held the floor. Now that he was dying, you would have thought that folk would show some restraint. After all, he could be no threat to them now. But they were as maliciously brutal as the Sanhedrin had been.

And the Sanhedrin hadn't gone away. They were there and enjoying their moment. Their fear of all Jesus' claims was at an end. He had broken their Sabbaths, blasphemed their religion and questioned their integrity. But now it was safe to mock. He had saved others, but was unable to save himself. They cast aspersions on his trust in God as well as his claim to be God's Son. Not even God wanted to save him! This taunting went on and on. Religious human beings degraded the Saviour and his claims. They could afford to say they would believe if he came down from the cross. But they never would and never did. They always shifted their ground and invented some other excuse.

Even the soldiers and the two bandits joined in, agreeing with the sentiments expressed by the Sanhedrin. Yes, if he was the Messiah why didn't he save the three of them? Jesus in his capacity as Saviour was maligned by everyone. The truth was that if he had saved himself then, he could never have saved any one.

Suddenly, just before noon, there was an unexpected turn of events. One of the robbers rebuked the other. He confessed that both of them were condemned justly, but not that man in the middle who had done nothing wrong. Addressing Jesus, he asked him to remember him in his kingdom. This prayer, as amazing in its faith as it was in its penitence, must have been like music to Jesus' ears. The man was not humouring him or being hostile. He was speaking believingly about Jesus' kingdom, and the fact that after death his existence would continue. Jesus' prompt reply would have been received gladly in the heart of any repentant sinner. 'I tell you the truth, today you will be with me in paradise.' It was a promise. Folk could mock him as the saviour and king. But he was still saving others on the basis of his kingdom.

And then Jesus was able to talk to his mother and with John who were standing quite near. They were to be mother and son now. So John took her to live with him.

Three hours of darkness
Matthew 27:45-56, Mark 15:33-41, Luke 23:44-49, John 19:28-37

At noon the sun stopped shining and dense darkness lasted for three hours. This was far longer than an eclipse of the sun. And it affected the whole country. In that period, nothing was said, but something extraordinary was happening. And as the darkness was just about over, Jesus, using the words of Psalm 22:1 cried out 'My God, my God, why have you forsaken me?' He was giving expression to his experience of spiritual desolation which was about to end.

Listening to his words were some curious observers who thought that something was about to happen. In the language of the time, the words 'My God' sounded like 'Eloi', and these people, consistent with Jewish beliefs, thought that Jesus was calling on Elijah presumably to introduce the Messianic era. They waited to see what would transpire. So when Jesus said he was thirsty one of the men showed him some consideration and offered him a sponge soaked in cheap wine on the end of a stalk of hyssop. Jesus took it. But Elijah did not appear to take him down from the cross. Jesus spoke again. 'It is finished!' 'Father, into your hands I commit my spirit.' And with that loud cry he died. It was not a sigh or a whimper. He did not die from slow exhaustion.

But those inquisitive spectators were mistaken. Nothing was *about to* happen involving Elijah. John the Baptist had already fulfilled all of those expectations. He had been the promised 'Elijah'. Jesus had said so in his teaching. Jesus' words indicated that something momentous, far reaching and grander had *already* taken place in the darkness of desolation. This was the greatest of all spiritual transactions. Jesus had faced the righteous anger of God, and borne the penalty of our sins in his own body. Simon Peter would later express it like this: 'He committed no sin, and no deceit was found in his mouth. When they hurled their insults at him, he did not retaliate; when he suffered, he made no threats. Instead, he entrusted himself to him who judges justly. He himself bore our sins in his body on the tree, so that we might die to sins and live for righteousness; by his wounds you have been healed' (1 Peter 2:22-24).

The desolation Jesus experienced had been because his Father had treated him as the offender instead of us. The apostle Paul declared that 'God made him (Christ) who had no sin to be sin for us, so that in him we might become the righteousness of God' (2 Corinthians 5:21). He also said that 'Christ redeemed us from the curse of the law by becoming a curse for us, for it is written: "Cursed is everyone who is hung on a tree." He redeemed us in order that the blessing given to Abraham might come to the Gentiles through Christ Jesus, so that by faith we might receive the promise of the Spirit' (Galatians 3:13-14).

As we have already noted, the cup he said he had to drink was the curse of the law as he was made a curse over us (to protect us); the baptism he endured forged a way of deliverance *through* the judgment; and the ransom price he paid *for* us was his own life. This was the way he would save his people from their sins.

The gospel writers were eager to show that the death of Jesus triggered at least three blessings: access to God, life from God and divine illumination. The tearing of the temple curtain signified the removal of the separation between God and the people. Approaching God was not dependent on religion but on Jesus' death. The rock splitting earthquake that opened the graves emphasised God's power to give life to the dead. And the Roman officer who had been there all along and had watched Jesus die saw the light and spoke up. Jesus had been a good man and was God's son. His mockery had changed to praise. Petronius is the name tradition gives this centurion. He took his place as a believer just like the robber.

The Jewish authorities were still concerned about religious and ritual niceties, however. They wanted everything sorted before the start of the Sabbath. The soldiers broke the legs of the two criminals. But because Jesus had died, they did not break his legs. John interpreted this as a fulfilment of Exodus 12:46 in which God had given instructions about the Passover lamb that no bones should be broken. But a soldier did plunge a spear into Jesus' side causing blood and water to stream out. Again John related this to the scripture. Zechariah 12:10 recorded that people would look at the one whom they pierced.

Jesus buried
Matthew 27:57-66, Mark 15:42-47, Luke 23:50-56, John 19:38-42

Two men of quite high standing, Joseph and Nicodemus, took responsibility for burying Jesus' body, officially sanctioned by Pilate. Joseph from Arimathea in Judea was a member of the Sanhedrin but had not voted in favour of their action against Jesus. His hope for the kingdom of God led him to be a follower of Jesus, but fear forced him to keep it secret. Nicodemus was a teacher of the law and one of those Pharisees who thought well of Jesus. Both of these men now made their stand. Joseph provided the tomb and enough linen cloth while Nicodemus brought enough myrrh and aloes to prepare the body for burial. They did not have to move the body far as Joseph's tomb was in a garden close to the place of crucifixion. So they laid Jesus to rest and rolled a boulder at the entrance to the tomb.

Noting carefully all of this were some Galilean women who had travelled south with Jesus. Nobody had taken much interest in them up till now. But they had been there to witness the death of their master, and were keen to do what they could, so they returned to where they were staying to prepare some spices and perfumes – that was the least they felt they could do. Then the Sabbath arrived and everything went quiet.

Not quite everything. Whereas the grief and depression of the disciples had blocked out all Jesus' teaching about his resurrection, the chief priests and Pharisees were defensive. They remembered that Jesus had taught he would rise again after three days. He had made no secret that the sign given to his contemporaries was the sign of Jonah the prophet. Just as Jonah was three days inside the great fish, so the Son of Man would be three days in the grave. The Jewish leaders were concerned that if the disciples stole the body, they could well use the empty grave as evidence that Jesus was raised from the dead. Deceivers bred deceivers. They took their concerns to Pilate. So they had the tomb sealed and a guard posted there for three days.

And that it would have appeared was that.

Messiah's resurrection

Matthew 28:1-15, Mark 16:1-8, Luke 24:1-12, John 20:1-10

The story was not over, however. From the four records we have, we can get a reasonably accurate picture of the events relating to the resurrection of Jesus. All four accounts were written from different perspectives, and are all valid; none of them provides a continuous free flowing uninterrupted narrative, however, but all of them blend with the overall story. It's as if each author had entered a series of bulleted notes in a diary.

The empty tomb

It would seem that two of those Galilean women, Mary Magdalene and Mary the mother of James, were rather restless. So before the Sabbath was over, that is sometime before 6 p.m. on the Saturday (Matthew 28:1, RV) they came to the tomb just to see it. There was nothing to report. The tomb would have been guarded, and all seemed normal. On Saturday evening after 6 p.m. they with Salome were able to buy extra spices in the city (Mark 16:1).

Nobody was there to witness the earthquake in the early hours of Sunday morning when it was still dark (Matthew 28:2-4). But the guards would later give their report to the chief priests who had to create a counter story. Angelic activity, so prominent at Messiah's birth, was prominent now. The angel rolled the stone away and sat on it, driving fear into the guards. The guards and the angel were gone before any women came.

Mary Magdalene was the first to arrive at the tomb. It was still dark (John 20:1) but she was able to note that the stone was moved. She was joined at sunrise by the other women (Mark 16:2-3, Luke 24:1-3) who had come to anoint the body of Jesus. They had realised that the large boulder at the tomb's entrance posed a problem but decided they would surmount that hurdle when they came to it. Before they arrived at the tomb, they could see that it wasn't a problem any longer. So the women entered the tomb. But there was no sign of Jesus' body.

It would appear from John 20:2 that at this point, Mary Magdalene left the other women at the tomb to report to Peter and John. She had seen nothing more than the entrance stone moved away and an empty tomb, and she assumed that there had been a grave robbery. So she told the apostles that some group had taken the Lord's body from the tomb and put it who knew where. She spoke as if she was representing the other women. At that moment she really did not know what was going on.

The message of the angels

Meanwhile, back at the tomb, not long after Mary had departed, the other women were taken aback, alarmed at the presence of a young man in a white robe sitting on the right side (Matthew 28:5-8, Mark 16:4-8, Luke 24:4-8). What on earth was he doing there? Then, suddenly two other dazzling figures were standing beside them, angels in the form of men. The women were understandably frightened until the angels spoke. And they were able to remember and later relate what they said.

First they were given the news that Jesus the crucified Nazarene had been raised to life. The women were shown where Jesus had been laid to rest and then were reminded that he had foretold his betrayal, death and resurrection on the third day. Yes, the light began to dawn as their memories were activated to recall Jesus' words. Then they were given instructions to tell his disciples, and particularly Peter, that they would see the risen Lord in Galilee. The women were shaking, bewildered and still a little afraid. But when joyful excitement became their main emotion they made a beeline for the eleven disciples. Mary Magdalene would still have been with the apostles. But this group of women that included Mary the mother of James, Salome and Joanna had better news to tell. The disciples, however, found their story incredible and their initial reaction was to dismiss it as nonsense (Luke 24:9-11).

The sensible thing, however, was to check out this story of an empty tomb and the angelic message (Luke 24:12, John 20:3-10). John who got to the tomb first just peered in. Peter went in to observe the arrangement of the linen cloths. John then joined him and was the first to believe the women's story. They then left. As yet, the risen Lord had appeared to nobody, however. This was about to change.

Jesus' appearances

The women who had reported to the apostles that the tomb was empty had followed Peter and John back to the tomb but at a more sedate pace. These would be the first to report that they saw Jesus alive.

Mary Magdalene was the first (Mark 16:9-11, John 20:11-18). This was her testimony. Distraught, she had looked into the tomb as Peter and John had done. It was then that she saw the angels that the other women had spoken about. She gave them the reason why she was so upset. It was because some group had moved the body and she couldn't find it. Then, intuitively, she sensed a presence behind her, and a man asked her why she was crying and who it was she was looking for. She assumed this man was the gardener, but when the man addressed her by her name, the light dawned. It was the Master. Jesus gave her the task of telling the disciples of his forthcoming ascension of Jesus to heaven. She was able now to say she had seen the Lord. But there was still a lot of unbelief to break down.

The other women also testified to seeing the risen Jesus (Matthew 28:9-10) as they left the tomb. They worshipped him. And Jesus repeated the message of the angel that he would meet his brothers in Galilee.

By now, the Jewish leaders were assimilating the reports of the guards (Matthew 28:11-15). They formulated a story for all to stick to, that under the cover of darkness, while the guards slept, the disciples had stolen the body. This was to become the accepted Jewish line to explain the disappearance of the body.

All of this took place on the Sunday morning.

In the afternoon, Jesus appeared to two of his followers going home to Emmaus (Mark 16:12-13, Luke 24:13-32). Their testimony was that the risen Lord joined them *incognito*, and a conversation soon ensued regarding the tragedy of the last three days. They told him the reason they were sad: that Jesus of Nazareth, a prophet mighty in deed and word before God and all the people, had been betrayed, condemned and crucified, and with his death all their hopes of redemption had vanished. But they were confused as well as sad – they related to him how they had heard reports that some women had been to his tomb, found it empty, and talked about seeing a vision of angels who said he was alive. True, part of their story had been verified, but no one had yet said they had seen the Lord alive. At this point Jesus began to explain to them that the scriptures had prophesied that the Messiah was destined to be a suffering Messiah before entering his glory. Messiah was the theme of the scriptures as far back as Moses and through all the prophets. Jesus' words so captivated and warmed their hearts that when the daylight started to fade, they invited him in for a meal. They soon recognised him – but then he was gone; so they hurried back the seven miles to Jerusalem (Luke 24:33-35), where on that Sunday evening they were able to share their story with the apostles and at the same time hear the confirmatory news that Jesus had appeared to Simon Peter (1 Corinthians 15:5).

But the evening was not over yet (Mark 16:14, Luke 24:36-43, John 20:19-25). Jesus made an appearance there and then, behind closed doors, and announced his presence with the words 'Peace unto you.' He needed to address their doubt and hardness of heart, and emphasised the point that he was not a ghostly apparition, but had real flesh and bones. He showed them his hands, feet and side, and their unbelief evaporated to be replaced by great joy. He even ate a piece of broiled fish. Then he commissioned them. He was sending them as the Father had sent him. Symbolically, he breathed over them, that their ministry of proclaiming forgiveness would be empowered by the Holy Spirit. Thomas, one of the twelve, was missing and when the others told him that they had seen the Lord he did not believe them. But a week later, in a similar setting, Jesus singled him out, and gave him the evidence he needed, so that he confessed Jesus as his Lord and God (John 20:26-31).

A little while later Jesus met seven of the disciples at the Sea of Galilee (John 21). This meeting was to prepare and commission Peter for his coming ministry. Jesus spoke the language of friendship, restoration and commission. Their night of fishing had ended in frustration with no fish caught, and when Jesus appeared as day was breaking they failed at first to recognise him. He told them to fish on the right side as a deliberate reminder of the time he had first called them as disciples. Again, the resultant catch was just as miraculous and Peter couldn't get to Jesus quick enough. The group had breakfast together. The risen Jesus presided at this breakfast just as he had at the last supper.

Jesus needed to address the issue of Peter's commitment and love and scrutinise the claim he had once made to be the most dedicated of all the disciples. Did Peter really love Jesus whatever it cost? In reply Peter twice used the word for friendship. Jesus then taught him that committed loyalty to Jesus would be shown by shepherding Jesus' flock and that if Peter was to meet that challenge he would be exposed to serious opposition and meet a violent death. It was in that light that Jesus reissued the call to Peter to follow him. Peter indeed would rise to the challenge never to forget this message (2 Peter 1:13-14). In his first letter he showed that he had assimilated and applied some basic principles of discipleship (1 Peter 2:20-21, 5:1-4).

Still in Galilee, Jesus met with the eleven disciples as arranged (Matthew 28:16-20). As the risen Lord all authority was his. As his servants they were commissioned to make disciples of all nations, baptizing them in the one name of the triune God, the Father, the Son and the Holy Spirit. They were to teach what he had commanded with a view to their obedience. He promised them his abiding presence to the very end of the age.

A little later at Jerusalem he was to underline the nature of their task (Luke 24:44-49, Acts 1:3-8). He spoke to them extensively about the kingdom of God. This was the priority. Then Jesus strengthened their faith in the context of the Scriptures. He reminded them that the Scriptures were about him, and that he was the fulfilment of the Law of Moses, the Psalms and the writings of the prophets. He then opened their minds to understand those Scriptures in terms of his death and resurrection. His summary was concise: that it was imperative that the

Messiah suffer and rise from death three days later (Hosea 6:2). Then Jesus delegated them, as the witnesses of those events, to proclaim in his name to all nations the message of repentance and the forgiveness of sins. They could start this new work after they were empowered by the Holy Spirit with power from on high. This was the baptism of spiritual power.

The last the disciples saw of Jesus was at his Ascension (Luke 24:50-53). In the area around Bethany, near the Mount of Olives, he blessed his people, and it was in the act of blessing them that he ascended to heaven. They became people of worship, joy and praise.

This is the information we are given of the resurrection of Jesus Christ – the discovery of an empty tomb was accompanied by the messages given by angels and crowned with several appearances of the risen Lord. The whole scenario would continue to be challenged and dismissed by unbelievers. But what was incontestable to all was that the disciples were transformed men. No longer were they deserters who cowered in fear of the authorities. They became courageous witnesses who would even face down the threats of persecution and death as they proclaimed a living Lord. Even their enemies noticed the change and failed to silence them. If, as was the charge, they had stolen the body of Jesus and hidden it somewhere, then they would have known he was dead. No one would sacrifice and die for something they knew was a lie. The truth was that the disciples at first were as bewildered as everyone else by what God was doing.

And it will not do to dismiss the whole matter as propaganda invented by writers. If it was propaganda, we would have to say that it wasn't very well thought out. In that society, for example, the testimony of women would have been completely discounted. Anyone who was concocting a story would never have made it dependent upon such a source. The same argument would apply to the reports of Messiah's birth given by shepherds. If the gospel writers had invented the story and wanted people to believe it, they would have appealed to different sources.

People of faith have therefore concluded that the records before us are as they are because that was the way it happened.

CHAPTER 10

The Long term Significance of Messiah's Mission

The author of the fourth gospel deliberately remains anonymous referring to himself as 'the disciple whom Jesus loved' or 'another disciple'. A group of believers, possibly the leadership of the church in Ephesus, who endorsed its circulation, regarded this person as a reliable eyewitness (21:20-24). He was present at the last Passover meal (13:23), was entrusted with looking after the mother of Jesus after the crucifixion (19:27) and was one of the seven disciples by the Sea of Galilee (21:1). He seems to have known Jerusalem well having had access to the palace of the high priest (18:15) and was aware of the deliberations of the Sanhedrin (7:45-52, 11:47-53, 12:10). The longest Christian tradition identifies him as John, the apostle.

The gospel is a theological argument with reference to Jesus' life. There are four clear parts to it, all of which are loaded with doctrinal content.

Chapter 1 is a prologue.

Chapters 2-12 refer to the public ministry of Jesus in Jerusalem, Judea, Samaria and Galilee.

In these two sections there is a fair amount of narrative, but it is carefully selected to include or introduce conversations Jesus took part in or discourses he gave. These sometimes merge with the author's comments.

In the third section, chapters 13-17, the emphasis is almost entirely on the words of Jesus, either in his private ministry to his apostles or in prayer to his Father.

Chapters 18-21 give an account of his death, resurrection and resurrection appearances.

In John 20:30-31, the author was clear about his purpose: 'Jesus did many other miraculous signs in the presence of his disciples, which are not recorded in this book. But these are written that you may believe that Jesus is the Christ, the Son of God, and that by believing you may have life in his name.'

We are therefore invited to examine his written evidence, specifically relating to the *miraculous signs*. This evidence was intended to point to the claims of a *unique person*. Jesus was his human name, but in two significant ways he is presented as much more than just a man. The assertion is that he was the Christ (that is, the Messiah, God's anointed king) and the Son of God (one who shared the Divine nature). The author confessed that the evidence was compiled to encourage, feed and appeal to *faith* on the part of his readers, for it was faith in Jesus Christ as the Son of God that was the gateway to *life*.

These four themes – miraculous signs, a unique person, faith and life – are woven into the narrative throughout the book. They dominate the record of his public ministry.

The signs

The miraculous signs concerned cases that were as varied as they were unusual in the extreme and ranged from Jesus' control over things like water, bread, fish and sea to his authority over disease, disability, blindness and death. It was in the servants' obedient act of pouring that water was transformed into wine at a wedding at Cana in Galilee (2:1-11). To a nobleman in Capernaum who had come to Jesus on behalf of his sick son, Jesus from a long distance away announced his healing at the seventh hour which the father later confirmed to be borne out by the facts (4:43-54). It was not just a disability, but a man's long standing disability that Jesus cured at Jerusalem's pool of Bethesda. He had lain immobile there for thirty eight years (5:1-14). In Galilee it was a large multitude of several thousand that was fed by a lad's lunch of five loaves and two fishes (6:1-13). Then, a man who was not just blind, but blind from birth, had his eyesight restored by means of a mud pack and a face wash at the pool of Siloam (9:1-7). Lazarus was not just raised from death but called out of his grave after he had been buried for four days (11:1-44). These events were deliberately selected. They were distinctive and exclusive to Jesus.

A unique person

The argument from Jesus' public ministry (John 2-12)

All of these extraordinary signs were a central plank in the author's case. We are told, for example, that Jesus did what he did at the wedding at Cana in order to display a particular facet of his glory (2:11), and that after the crowd had been fed, people were coming to the conclusion that Jesus was the promised Prophet that Moses had spoken about (6:14).

In the case of the man healed at the pool of Bethesda on the Sabbath day, Jesus justified his activity by comparing it with the continuous work of God, uninterrupted by religious days. In doing this he referred to God as his Father. This led to a very nasty reaction from the Jewish authorities who saw his words as a claim to equality with God (5:18). Jesus did not correct their conclusion, but actually gave them more grist for their mill. He said that the Father had conferred on him a much greater power than physical healing which extended to his authority both to impart spiritual life and to execute ultimate judgement (5:20-26). He was the one who held in his hands people's destiny. In his capacity as the Son of Man he made the decision whether a man was blessed or judged (5:27). All of this teaching about his person sprang from the miracle he had performed.

The record of the healing of the man born blind led to similar repercussions as it clearly presented Jesus as the light of the world performing a divine work. The miracle was examined, inspected, assessed and even validated by people whose attitudes ranged from curiosity to antagonism. Neighbours noticed the change in someone whose congenital blindness up till then had dictated for so long that all he did was to sit helplessly and beg (9:8). But in a cynical and sustained challenge, the Jewish religious leaders dismissed the man's clear testimony as invalid – because it didn't tally with their prejudices. The miracle again had taken place on the Sabbath day. Jesus therefore could not have been from God because he broke the Sabbath (9:16). This argument concealed the more serious underlying issue that any person's voiced belief in Jesus as the Messiah meant their expulsion from the synagogue (9:18-23). Camps were forming for and against Jesus as the Messiah. As for the former blind man, his growing personal appreciation of and admiration for Jesus was obvious: first, he had referred to Jesus as 'the man they call Jesus'; then, when the Pharisees asked him intimidatingly his opinion of Jesus, he answered, 'He is a prophet'; then he saw Him as a godly man who did God's will, and, led by the direction of Jesus' question, he saw Him as someone to trust. Finally, when Jesus identified himself as the Son of Man, 'he worshipped him.' The whole episode was leading up to this distinct Messianic claim.

This was also the case with the sickness and death of Lazarus. It occurred, said Jesus, so that he as the Son of God would receive glory (11:4). He told Martha that he was the resurrection and the life and she responded that she believed him to be the Messiah and the Son of God who was to come into the world (11:25-27). And when, at the word of Jesus, Lazarus emerged from his tomb, Jesus the Lord of life and death became the object of people's attention and faith (11:45,48).

The deliberate link between these signs and the status of Jesus grows more obvious as we examine the text. It was recognised, for example, by the Jewish leader and open minded Pharisee Nicodemus. He and the group he represented had concluded that Jesus could not have done what he was doing if God were not with him. He therefore told Jesus he believed he was a teacher who had come from God (3:2). Also, at the Feast of Tabernacles in Jerusalem, a sizeable proportion of the crowd realised that the promised Messiah would not perform any more miracles than Jesus had done (7:31), and later in the same week would identify him as the Prophet and the Messiah (7:40-41). And when Jesus was asked directly by less sympathetic groups if he was the Messiah, he answered that his deeds spoke for him (10:25). His assertion was treated as blasphemy, for in their view it was tantamount to claiming deity (10:33).

The clear statements in the prologue (John 1)

Of course, if we had started at the beginning of the book, we would not at all be surprised at any of the above material. We would see that it was really a development of what John had written in his prologue as he set out his stall. Testimonies to the uniqueness of Jesus were given by people who had encountered him.

The author's perspective: Jesus was the Word of God and the Light of God (1:1-18)

Spoken words communicate a person's thoughts. Thoughts are the source of words. Jesus as God's word, according to the author, expressed the nature and mind of God. But this general statement carried detailed implications which when unpacked and understood were quite astounding. For example, he says that Jesus as the 'Word' antedated time. When the beginning began, he already was. He was associated with God in perfect fellowship and shared glory with the Father before the world began (17:5). This was the result of nothing other than equality. The visible complex universe owed its origin to the creative mind of God, apart from whose Word nothing could exist. The eternal 'Word' was the agent in the work of creation.

It was no less a being than this eternal Word who became the incarnate Word – that is, the one who was with God came to be with man as he voluntarily 'made his dwelling' or 'pitched his tent' among us. His humanity was full and real, but he did not stop being what he always was. God cannot stop being God, because that would mean he would deny himself. Therefore he displayed God's glory as the one who lived in that unique Father/Son relationship. At the same time that he lived in the world, he also continued to live in His Father (1:18, 14:10-11). In this way he was the personal revelation of the invisible God. His life in human society was an explanation and interpretation of the being and nature of God. He made God known. And in so doing he was a reservoir of grace and truth for humanity.

This was the author's rationale behind his assertion that this Word was the essence of life. Humanity's life was a derived and dependent life, but not his. He was the source of life for all of humanity. As such he brought light to people who were encompassed and conditioned by the spiritual darkness and death caused by sin. In and of itself, darkness could not threaten light, but had to give way to it. However, because mankind was spiritually blind and sinfully rebellious, the prophet John had to come to awaken people to their need of God's revelation concerning the true light. Even so, Messiah's own people would still shut their eyes and turn him away.

John the Baptist's witness: Jesus was the Lamb of God and the Son of God (1:19-34)

John couldn't have been clearer when asked about his own identity. He was not the Messiah, or a reincarnation of Elijah, or the prophet like Moses. He was the promised 'voice' preparing the way of the Lord. And one of John's vocal announcements was made the very next day as Jesus approached: 'Look, the Lamb of God, who takes away the sin of the world.' There was an issue to be recognised here. Mankind's great and universal problem was its sin against God that had formed a barrier between man and God. But this declaration about Jesus' mission was that through the action of the Lamb of God that barrier would be removed and carried away – thereby opening up access to the God whose arm was not shortened that he could not save. It would seem that John combined two Old Testament images in this announcement – that of the Passover Lamb and that of the scapegoat on the Day of Atonement. The blood of the lamb on the doorposts meant that the people sheltering inside those houses were spared the judgment of death. The goat on the Day of Atonement carried the people's sins away into the desert. No one else was capable of doing what Jesus did in relation to the question of sin. Jesus is unique. In fact John went on to say that he was the Son of God.

The disciples' testimony: Jesus was the Messiah, King of Israel, Son of Man (1:37-51)

Andrew acted on the word of John the Baptist, the result being that he had a long session with Jesus, after which he told his brother, Simon Peter, that he had been with the Messiah. Philip, who also had spent time with Jesus in response to Jesus' invitation, then told Nathanael what he knew. And when Nathanael met Jesus he confessed him to be the Son of God and the King of Israel. Jesus confirmed to Nathanael that he, as the Son of Man, was the means of access to an open heaven.

So in this very first chapter the claims concerning Jesus Christ are set forth as the Word who is both God and man, the Life, the Light, the Lamb, the Son of God, the Messiah, King of Israel and the Son of Man.

The call for faith

Everything that Jesus did, whether miraculous or ordinary, was according to the will of his Father and in his Father's name. He told a group of unbelieving Jews that his deeds and the way he behaved should have been enough for them to believe (10:24-28); he told his disciples the same thing (14:10-14; 15:23,24).

When faith followed the evidence, the focal point of the evidence became the focal point of faith. The starting point had to be acknowledging and agreeing with the evidence, but the faith that the author had in mind was far more than mental assent to the truth of a proposition. At some point it became faith *in* Jesus Christ.

There were so many illustrations of this principle that it's worth making a list: at the wedding at Cana his disciples put their faith in him (2:11); at the Passover at Jerusalem many people were impressed and believed in his name (2:22-23); when the woman Jesus met in Samaria told the folk in the town that she had met the Messiah, many Samaritans believed in him because of her testimony, and more followed when they heard Jesus for themselves (4:39,41-42), confessing that he was the Saviour of the world; the nobleman who first acted on Jesus' word later witnessed his whole household believing (4:43-54); at the Feast of Tabernacles in Jerusalem, more impressed people put their faith in Jesus as the Messiah (7:31);

after the man's sight was restored, Jesus pressed him with the question as to whether he believed in him as the Son of Man (9:35-38); when Jesus returned to the place where John had been baptising in the early days, many people remembered John's testimony about Jesus and believed in Jesus (10:40-41); before and after the raising of Lazarus, Martha and other Jews faced the same issue of faith in him as the Messiah and Son of God (11:25-27,45,47-48, 12:9-11); and at the conclusion of his public ministry there were several among the Jewish leaders (Nicodemus and Joseph of Arimathea for example) who secretly believed in him (12:42).

All of these were illustrations of how the evidence that was seen led to faith in *Him* as a person. This, according to the gospel has several constituent parts:

Faith is a welcome

It means a welcome given to Jesus as the Word of God and as the Light of God. The *eternal* Word who was with God became the *incarnate* Word in the world so that he could become the *received* Word in people's minds and lives. Society in general, the nation he belonged to and even his own brothers failed to welcome Him. But some did – and it is here that we have our first definition of faith. Those who 'received' him were the same as those who 'believed' in him (1:12).

Many students at Aberystwyth University attend St Michael's church. At the start of the academic year, parents attend for a Sunday having brought their sons or daughters to Wales with all their stuff. On one occasion, a parent commented to Ollie Baker, a member of the welcome team, that the church was different from what he had envisaged it to be. She replied, 'That's because Jesus is here.' He responded, 'But isn't Jesus in every church?' To which Ollie said, 'But here we want him.'

Faith in Jesus was expressed in its welcome for Jesus. Some people wanted him; many didn't.

Faith is a focus

It means a focus on Jesus as the Son of God and as the Lamb of God. Faith becomes fascinated with Jesus. It could even be described as a fixation on Him. Jesus used an Old Testament incident to make this point to Nicodemus: he said, 'Just as Moses lifted up the snake in the desert, so the Son of Man must be lifted up, that everyone who believes may have in him eternal life' (3:14,15). It was a reference to Numbers 21.

Fiery snakes had been sent as a judgement on the people. But Moses was told to set a bronze model of a snake upon a standard so that victims of the snakebites might look toward it and live. The remedy was related to this uplifted bronze serpent made in the likeness of a fiery snake. The people were not told to run, kill the snakes, or to suck out the poison, but simply to look at the bronze model of the very thing that caused the problem. In making his analogy, Jesus substituted the word 'believe' for 'look'. The apostle Paul would teach that God made the sinless Jesus 'to be sin for us' (2 Corinthians 5:21) and sent His own Son 'in the likeness of sinful flesh, and for sin,' and thus 'condemned sin in the flesh' (Romans 8:3). Peter said the same thing in different words: 'He bore our sins in His own body on the tree' (1 Peter 2:24).

Faith is a partaking

The sequel to the feeding of the multitude in Galilee (6:1-70) was a discourse about partaking of Jesus as the bread of life. This, in Jesus' analogy, was equated with believing in the one God had sent (6:29). This claim started a discussion revolving around the miraculous feeding of the Israelites in the wilderness with the manna, the bread from heaven. But the Jewish take on history was tending to obscure the point Jesus wished to make. Its value lay in the fact that it provided a material picture of a greater spiritual reality. The Jews should stop thinking in terms of Moses, the manna and wilderness survival, and see the Father rather than Moses, Jesus rather than manna and eternal life rather than desert endurance (6:32-33). Jesus was the bread of God from heaven who gave life to the world, and in the same way that the survival of the people in the desert revolved around 'eating', so the way to enjoy eternal life was all to do with believing. Eating was a necessary and personal activity for the life and health of the body. Believing was an equally necessary and personal activity for the life and health of the spirit. The eating and digesting of food impacted on the physical body.

Faith as a spiritual receptive partaking of Jesus impacted on the soul and personality.

The same point was made in John 7 when Jesus attended the Feast of Tabernacles. As the celebrations were coming to an end, Jesus publicly announced that all who were spiritually thirsty should come to him and drink. He was talking again about faith as a partaking. He would give the Holy Spirit who is likened to 'streams of living water.' The alternative translation of John 7:37-38 in the NIV makes the point more clearly: 'Jesus stood and said in a loud voice, If anyone is thirsty, let him come to me. And let him drink, who believes in me.'

Faith, then, is far more than assent to and acceptance of the proposition that God exists. Yet this is what a lot of folk mean when they speak of faith – they believe that someone is there. To reduce it to this is misleading and farcical. It is like someone who does not want to invest any money or borrow any money, but regularly calls in to the bank to tell the bank manager that he exists and to assure him he's doing a good job; or who visits his local medical practitioner not to get treatment but just to say he believes the name on the doctor's door is correct.

John was concerned that we get it right.

Eternal life

The consistent testimony of Jesus, both publicly and privately, was that faith directed towards and placed in him resulted in life.

These were his words when he taught the public: 'whoever hears my word and believes him who sent me has eternal life … he has crossed over from death to life' (5:24); 'I am the living bread that came down from heaven. If anyone eats of this bread, he will live forever' (6:51); 'I am the light of the world. Whoever follows me will never walk in darkness, but will have the light of life' (8:12); 'My sheep listen to my voice; I know them, and they follow me. I give them eternal life, and they shall never perish' (10:27,28).

Jesus repeated this in private to individuals: he said to Nicodemus that 'the Son of Man must be lifted up, that everyone who believes may have in him eternal life' (3:14,15); to the Samaritan woman at a well, he gave this promise, 'Whoever drinks the water I give him will never thirst. Indeed, the water I give him will become in him a spring of water welling up to eternal life' (4:14); and to Martha who was grieving over the death of her brother he said, 'I am the resurrection and the life. He who believes in me will live, even though he dies; and whoever lives and believes in me will never die' (11:25,26).

The more we pause to think about the whole concept of life, whether vegetative, animal, human or spiritual, the more amazing it appears. Those who accept the Bible believe that all forms of life owe their existence to God. The life Jesus was talking about was spiritual life – by which he meant nothing less than a sharing in the life of God revealed in the Messiah which was dependent on a relationship with God on the basis of faith. 'Whoever believes in the Son has eternal life, but whoever rejects the Son will not see life' (3:36). It is called eternal life because it is a quality of life that belongs to the eternal God.

Eternal life was through new birth

The author asserted: 'Yet to all who received him, to those who believed in his name, he gave the right to become children of God' (1:12). This was therefore spiritual life that someone had by virtue of being spiritually 'born'. This 'birth' followed as a result of the welcome shown to Messiah. God granted those persons the privileged right to become what they were not before – children of God in the full spiritual sense, not just creatures that depended on Him for physical existence. The author continued by saying that becoming God's spiritual child was not related to natural birth, any physical process, human decision or inheritance. It was dependent upon a person's welcome shown to Messiah Jesus.

This point was developed in Jesus' interview with Nicodemus who wanted to check out the conclusions about Jesus he had reached so far. But very early in their discussion, as Nicodemus was proceeding cautiously, Jesus declared that no one could participate in the kingdom of God unless he was born 'from above' (3:3). He meant that a major transformation was required for a person to adapt to the kingdom's new conditions, and birth, as the means of entrance to the world, was an appropriate concept to express this. Nicodemus acknowledged that he had been conditioned by a rigid religious outlook when he replied, in effect, that it was a heavy demand of a man whose habits and beliefs were fixed by age to change tack radically. He was what he was. To change now spiritually was as impossible as crawling back into the womb physically. He was familiar with the notion of 'rebirth' for Gentile proselytes to Judaism, but not with the idea that a pedigree Jew had to be reborn. But Jesus was adamant – Nicodemus must grasp the truth that spiritual rebirth, 'of water and the Spirit', was essential to entrance into the kingdom of God. Jesus may have been referring to the preaching and baptism of John the Baptist which included confession of sin and repentance which the Pharisees had rejected. It may also be that both 'water' and 'wind' are symbols for the Spirit of God. The point made was that there was a sharp contrast between flesh and Spirit as the author had already said in his prologue (1:13). The realm of flesh was confined – it reproduced only its own kind. If Nicodemus were to rule out the new birth by the Spirit, he was stuck with his religious legalism and external conformity. He needed an inner change by the direct act of God.

Eternal life was God's gift

In his short ministry Jesus met all sorts of people from the religiously cantankerous to the intellectually curious. As he travelled north to Galilee he was about to meet someone who was spiritually hungry. The people of Samaria, originally a mixed race, had a 700 year history, long enough to establish for themselves a national identity, which in their eyes was as good if not better than that of the neighbouring Jews in Judea. Samaritans were religious, yes; but the strict proponents of Judaism in Jesus' day saw no good whatsoever in them, and hotly opposed them. The average Jew simply ignored them and kept out of their way. Their relationship was one of simmering hatred, which on occasions boiled over. Jesus was well aware of the hate and the tension, but also aware that the religion of the Jews had deteriorated to the point of inadequacy.

Jesus did not share the current orthodox Jewish attitudes and values but he did not take sides. So, when he met a Samaritan woman he had no position to defend. For her, the meeting was just a chance encounter with no importance attached. In fact she was quite off hand at first.

Yes, he may have been fatigued with his journey, but that didn't lessen her surprise at this Jew's total disregard of current prejudice. He didn't seem to mind becoming ceremonially unclean by using a Samaritan drinking bowl. This was true because Jesus was focussed on two issues he saw as of supreme importance, and that what why as a Jewish man he wanted to talk to a Samaritan woman. The topics of conversation proved interesting and intriguing: they always are when he sets the agenda.

He kicked off with, 'If you knew the gift of God and who it is that asks you for a drink, you would have asked him and he would have given you living water.' He wanted to discuss the question of *the gift of God* and the question of his own *identity.* For he knew that when a person was enlightened as to those two questions a sequence of blessing followed. Light led to desire, and desire led to request and request led to reception. But as yet the woman knew nothing of either issue. She did not know that the Jew was the anointed one. She did not know that the gift of God was the Spirit of God as an internal spring of water within (4:14). She thought the Jew was talking about some labour saving device.

As Jesus' disciples we now know and rejoice that the whole gift, which Jesus likened to living water, was nothing less than the gift of the Holy Spirit with eternal life and the forgiveness of sins (Acts 2:38, 10:45, 11:17).

The light started to dawn for the Samaritan woman when Jesus mentioned her life story. She began to wonder why he was interested and how he knew all about her (4:18,29,39). He must be a prophet. But she couldn't sort it out, so she opted to change the topic to the more general topic of worship sites which she felt she could discuss on equal terms. But that didn't go too well either because he didn't seem interested in fighting the Jewish corner. He talked of the Father God to be worshipped in spirit and truth, which was a matter of the heart and not of geographical location or cultural emphasis. Her mind was still ticking over. She thought she was ending the conversation by saying – well who knows! Only Messiah yet to come can tell us all things (4:25). At that point Jesus revealed his identity: 'I who speak to you am he.' He had already started to display some special knowledge when he told her what he knew of her past, and when he spoke so clearly about his identity, light shone into her soul.

She started to appreciate the life as a gift. As one of Messiah's spiritual sheep, she had heard his voice, become a believer and even then begun to follow him. To such Jesus promised eternal life as a gift. Jesus explained this to Jews who rejected him: '… you do not believe because you are not my sheep. My sheep listen to my voice; I know them, and they follow me. I give them eternal life, and they shall never perish; no one can snatch them out of my hand. My Father, who has given them to me, is greater than all; no one can snatch them out of my Fathers hand' (10:26-29).

Eternal life was sustained by Messiah

Alongside the truths that eternal life was the gift of God the Father through new birth by the Holy Spirit we must place the truth that the essence of that life was Messiah himself. This is stated succinctly in the prologue: 'In him was life, and that life was the light of men' (1:4); later Jesus would combine the same two concepts and say, 'I am the light of the world. Whoever follows me will never walk in darkness, but will have the light of life' (8:12). The truth is repeated and expanded in John's first letter: '… this is the testimony: God has given us eternal life, and this life is in his Son. He who has the Son has life; he who does not have the Son of God does not have life' (1 John 5:11,12). Jesus is its source.

This is why he spoke about himself as the living bread. 'I tell you the truth, he who believes has everlasting life. I am the bread of life. Your forefathers ate the manna in the desert, yet they died. But here is the bread that comes down from heaven, which a man may eat and not die. I am the living bread that came down from heaven. If anyone eats of this bread, he will live forever' (6:47-51).

It was why Jesus spoke of himself as the source of the life of the Spirit: whoever was spiritually thirsty should get close enough to him to drink of the streams of life-giving water pouring from him. 'By this he meant the Spirit, whom those who believed in him were later to receive' (7:37-39).

It was why he described himself as the gate for the sheep. He said, 'I am the gate; whoever enters through me will be saved … the thief comes only to steal and kill and destroy; I have come that they may have life, and have it to the full' (10:7-10). And it was why he would say to Martha, 'I am the resurrection and the life. He who believes in me will live, even though he dies; and whoever lives and believes in me will never die' (11:25-26).

I trust we have done justice to John's case so far. What we have to see next is how this amazing fourfold theme was meant to impact upon his disciples' futures.

Faith's nature and implications
John 13–17

In the next section things moved on somewhat. As Jesus was preparing to return to his Father, he was concerned to prepare his people for their future without his physical presence. So in chapters 13–17 we have the specific teaching he gave to his disciples whom he now addressed and regarded as his personal friends. He was intent on establishing how faith in him would work out in their lives and what its implications would be.

Before we look at the details, notice how John's stated theme stayed consistent: the disciples were not to neglect the evidence concerning him as the unique one, evidence that was to be believed. He taught them with emphasis that He and His Father were one: he appealed to them to believe that he was in the Father and the Father in him, and he backed up that appealed with reference to the evidence (14:10-14).

There are several characteristics of the sort of faith Jesus was looking for. His words set the standard and act as a spirit level or plumb line. He was not asking the impossible or setting the bar too high. And yet over the centuries his words have been side lined or side stepped in the interests of a variety of religious emphases.

A faith that was expressed in humility like Jesus
John 13:1-30

Faith in Jesus Christ would identify willingly *with the servant spirit of Jesus*. This would not happen automatically. The lesson needed to be taught, and was best taught in a practical act. When Jesus washed his disciples' feet, he demonstrated his love for them in serving them. He was their example of greatness, yes; but the true greatness he envisaged revolved around the concept of service and not around status. He knew who he was and where he was going, and needed to prove nothing more about himself. But his disciples still needed enlightenment. So, having laid aside his outer clothing and with a towel around his waist, he proceeded to perform the most menial of tasks, washing and drying their feet. Every disciple received the service Jesus offered until he came to Peter who protested. But Jesus pointed out that failure to accept the service of foot washing was a rejection of the spirit of his mission. Their service to one another was both to be given readily and received thankfully by all of his followers.

Did they understand his action? If not, Jesus would explain. He was their recognised teacher and Lord whose action placed an obligation on them to follow his example of humility and service. For no servant was greater than his master. But knowing must lead to doing. If this teaching of Jesus was absorbed and applied, then whoever accepted the ones he sent accepted him, and in turn that meant acceptance of the Father.

Of course, it was quite possible for all of this to go over their heads. And there was among them one who would even eat at the same table as Jesus and still betray him for monetary profit. To Judas something else was far more important than this servant spirit. But it was the key to loyalty to Christ. No one is a true representative of Jesus without it.

A faith that prompted prayer in the name of Jesus
John 13:31 – 14:14

Prayer in the name of Jesus is prayer that *appreciates the influential role of Jesus.* After Judas had left the upper room, Jesus started a talk which was interrupted in turn by Peter, Thomas and Philip. Jesus dealt with their questions and each time resumed his main theme. The flow of what he was saying was that real faith would be expressed in their prayers to the Father in his name (14:13-14). To pray like this meant they were confessing their dependence on him.

With that in mind, he was at pains to teach them two related themes: that faith in Him would see Him as having both *influential honour in heaven* and *influential authority on earth* (13:31-35). On the one hand, he was about to return to his Father who would crown him with glory and honour; and on the other, his influence would continue on earth when his disciples showed the same love to each other that he had showed them. His new command to them was that they love one another as he had loved them. This was the evidence of being a disciple of Messiah.

The first interruption came in the form of Simon Peter's claim to be ready to accompany Jesus to death. Jesus pointed him back to reality and then resumed the first element of his theme – that he did indeed have influence in heaven, so much so that all of their apprehensions could be ousted and overwhelmed by their trust in him. After all, it was he who in going away would prepare places for them in the Father's house (heaven) and then return to welcome them to be where he was going to be. Their futures depended on him. It seems that in talking about heaven and his second coming Jesus was alluding to the idea of a bridegroom who came from his own home to take his betrothed bride back there with him. But all this would have been an empty platitude if Jesus did not have supremacy in heaven. Faith had to trust him and rely on him.

Thomas then spoke up; he was not at all clear as to where Jesus was going or the way there. So Jesus replied that all they needed was *him* – he was the way to the Father. But before he could continue his theme of trust in him Philip wanted Jesus to show them the Father. At this point Jesus stressed that the Father could do no more for them than what Jesus already meant to them, and was already committed to do for them – for there was such unity and solidarity between Jesus and the Father that it could be said he was the revelation of the Father. He gave an example: they had heard Him speak living words and seen Him do mighty and compassionate deeds; but those words and deeds were the result of the Father living in Him. Thus Jesus in his reply to Philip was getting back to and supporting the first part of his theme – that he had influential honour in heaven.

He then proceeded to the second part of his theme: that his authority on earth would continue. His people would be the channel and his Spirit the agent of that authority. But for this to happen it was vital for his disciples to engage in believing prayer. Being part of the apostolic group was not enough. They needed to examine themselves as to whether they really did believe in Jesus. Judas had already gone off to betray him, and of those who were left Peter would disown him, Thomas would doubt and all would desert. So Jesus needed to make clear to them that when he returned to the Father it would only be the ones who believed who would carry on his ministry (14:12).

Jesus then made it clear that the ministry that would continue through his apostles would belong to a superior category than that of physical healings. This is the meaning of the word translated as 'greater', a word which John used extensively. It did not refer to a bigger quantity or a better quality, but to something that was of a *higher classification*. There are many examples of its use: the sin of Caiaphas was classified as 'greater' because it was of a more serious nature than that of Pilate (19:11); the notion that Jesus was 'greater' than Jacob (4:12) and Abraham (8:53) referred to his loftier and superior status; the testimony to Jesus that he said was 'greater' than that of John the Baptist was evidence of a weightier sort in that it came from the Father (5:36); and the 'greater' love which led a man to lay down his life for his friends (15:13) was a different brand of love that was of a more resolute and committed nature.

Jesus was not promising that his followers would do better signs and miracles than he did. How could anyone compete with Jesus' calm control of nature or his instant, unaided and comprehensive healing of extreme cases with no medical support team? John's whole case was that the remarkable signs Jesus did proved his uniqueness. He would have undermined his argument if he meant these could be duplicated or improved on. This is not to say that God ever ceased his work of healing. He obviously has not. When he wills it nothing can stand in his way or thwart his sovereign wisdom. These same apostles would indeed do miracles in Jesus' name, empowered as they were by the Holy Spirit, but they were not greater than those done by Jesus.

In 5:20-25, Jesus said that there was 'a greater work' than his healing of the lame man (5:1-16). This was his right to bestow spiritual life and to act as the final judge of all. Healings belonged in the realm of the physical, the immediate and the local. But the apostolic ministry controlled by the Holy Spirit was of a spiritual, eternal and global nature – not least the ministry that resulted in man's reconciliation to God that included the blessing of the forgiveness of sins.

But all of this would depend on prayer to the Father in Jesus' name. They were dependent on Jesus. It meant that their praying was not to be self-seeking but for God's glory.

A faith that worked by love for Jesus
John 14:15-31

If faith is created in the first place when someone hears the proclamation concerning Jesus as Messiah (Romans 10:17), then it is sustained by a love for Jesus *that obeys and submits to him*. Such love is the energy of faith. And the whole process – of believing, loving and obeying – is facilitated and empowered by the Holy Spirit. Jesus had already established that there was solidarity between the Father and himself. Now he extended the truth of solidarity to include the third member of the Godhead, the person of the Holy Spirit who would replace Jesus in the lives of the disciples after he left. The Holy Spirit was indeed with them while Jesus was with them; but he would soon dwell within them on a permanent basis.

The same three verbs are used to describe the coming of the Holy Spirit that described the coming of Jesus: he *came*, meaning he had a necessary work to do that could only be done by his personal presence; he was *sent*, meaning he represented the authority of God; and he was *given*, meaning that he personified the grace of God. Jesus and the Holy Spirit were one in nature and purpose. The Holy Spirit would be to them all that Jesus had been. Through him they would still be inseparably linked to Jesus.

In response to Judas' request for clarification, Jesus summarised it. All of this meant that they were to love him in obeying his teaching. If they did he promised them that the Triune God would dwell in their inner beings. The teaching from God would not change. The Holy Spirit, like Jesus, would faithfully minister the Father's word to them. Jesus' influence and authority would indeed continue. And in accepting this development he promised them his peace.

A faith that led to fellowship with Jesus
John 15:1-17

The Father/Son/Spirit solidarity continues into John 15. First, there was Jesus' allegory of the vine with its branches, which the Father pruned. The disciples, like the branches of the vine, *were to abide in Jesus*, which was a vivid picture of maintaining fellowship with him. In this way they would be spiritually fruitful and bring glory to the Father. Of course, a grafted branch might not successfully take – so it would be cut off. It was dead. Probably Jesus here alluded to Judas Iscariot. The life coursing in the vine was the life of the Spirit which the disciples as the branches would partake of through their fellowship with Jesus. Spiritual fruit was the result of life. Paul spoke about bearing fruit to God (Romans 7:6), being fruitful in every good work (Colossians 1:10) and being filled with the fruit of righteousness (Philippians 1:11).

Fruit would grow in the atmosphere of his love. That was why Jesus spoke about obeying him, especially his command to love each other sacrificially. This was the secret of joy. It would mean being classed as his friends. And as his friends he promised that the Father would hear them when they prayed in his name.

A faith that would endure suffering for Jesus
John 15:18 – 16:6

Jesus wanted to make it clear that real faith in him would create a noticeable difference between those who followed him and those who did not. The result for his followers would be trouble. They would have to endure pressure, distress, anguish, suffering, hardships, affliction, trials, hatred and persecution – just as Jesus did. His followers belonged to him because he had chosen them. No longer did they belong to 'the world'.

The 'world' here does not refer to the design and beauty of creation or to the order of human society as originally created. It is a reference to the arrangement of a secular *system* that is organised by God's arch enemy, Satan, so that mankind in rejecting God's values adopts the alternative principles of force, greed, pride, selfishness, ambition and pleasure. These like a cancer infiltrate all sorts of social structures, whether political, commercial, religious, scientific, educational or cultural.

Jesus told the Roman governor that his kingdom was not of this world. If it had been, his followers would have resorted to force (John 18:36). But Jesus' kingdom was organised on the principle of faith and not force. He advocated virtues such as contentment, humility, godliness, service, duty and modesty. The world did not know God or his society; it rejected Jesus and was unsympathetic to his mission; it was a stranger to the Holy Spirit and to real peace; it hated Jesus and all who stood for righteousness. The world was the source and sphere of trouble for the Christian. It was a defiling agent (James 1:27, 2 Peter 1:4, 2 Peter 2:20). Someone who loved the world in this sense was in a different camp from someone who did the will of God. They were therefore not to be at all surprised if they felt hatred from secular society.

A faith that gave glory to Jesus
John 16:7-33

Jesus talked about the need to be *responsive to the control of the Holy Spirit.* The Holy Spirit was the divine helper. And his work through the church would be quite specific – he would consistently testify that society's unbelief was sin, that Jesus had always been right, and that the adversary Satan was condemned and doomed. In fact, the Holy Spirit would lead the community of Jesus in the truth that Jesus had already taught and which had come originally from the Father. He was not going to change the agenda. In this way the Holy Spirit would bring glory to Jesus.

And the disciples needed to be aware of this work of the Holy Spirit, because it would not be long before Jesus was to go away. They were about to go through a period of great insecurity as they were scattered by their fear of the opposition. Their grief at that time would be enjoyed by a society that thought they had got rid of Jesus for good. But Jesus said that their sorrow when he left them would not be permanent. It would rather be like labour pains – which were not nice but which had a purpose because they were a means to an end. Likewise, for them the end in sight was not one of grief but of joy. The whole point of Jesus' going was that the Spirit would come. And through the Spirit they were expected to pray to the Father in Jesus' name. The answers they then received to the prayers they offered would complete their joy. It was a sign of the Father's own love for them.

All of this teaching was designed to instil peace into the disciples' lives even in a society that just meant trouble for them. But the peace depended on whether they took to heart the teaching, especially those statements about the Father's love, the Spirit's help and the fact that Jesus had defeated the world. As Paul would put it, the mind controlled by the Spirit enjoyed life and peace (Romans 8:6).

When his people really appreciated the fact that Jesus had overcome the world, all issues would be seen in a completely different light. Jesus already stood in judgement over the rebellious system led by the devil, and had already promised that his adversary would be thrown out, thoroughly ejected as an unlawful intruder (John 12:31,32). Not only so, but people who were then enslaved by the system and its leader would find themselves drawn to Jesus when he was raised up from the earth in crucifixion. The apostle Paul counted himself among that number. He saw that his relationship with the world was ended by Messiah's cross. He taught that Jesus Christ had given himself for our sins in order to rescue us from the present evil age (Galatians 1:4) which explained his declared personal intention that he would only boast about the cross of our Lord Jesus Christ. It was through this that he had been crucified to the world and the world to him. The old relationship was dead (Galatians 6:14).

Jesus didn't belong to the world system. He didn't pray for it and spoke against it. He rejected its values, challenged its principles, opposed its prince and warned his people against it. For its part, the world didn't recognise him or understand Him; it hated him and crucified him. The world and God were completely incompatible. James would be very blunt when he wished to guide people's choices. He wrote that friendship with the world equalled hatred toward God. Any disciple faced with that choice would become aware of the guidance of the indwelling Holy Spirit who was a fierce protagonist for the glory of God (James 4:4-5).

At the 1982 Commonwealth games, both the Australian and Canadian teams in the four man swimming relay were guilty of infringements at different changeover points during the race. But the race was not stopped. If folk had only seen the last two lengths, they would presume that Australia had won easily with Canada a creditable second. But they would have been wrong. What seemed to be the case was not in fact the case. What the judges had noted during the race was announced at the end of it. Some members of the disqualified teams were completely innocent but still shared in the disappointment.

Christians today need to be reminded that the world system has already been disqualified by the Judge. The race goes on, however, and it *seems* that the world is far more impressive than Messiah's followers. But belonging to the world means belonging to the wrong team. The world is in fact passing away like a procession going down the street and out of sight around the corner, but it's the one who does God's will who will abide forever. The glory belongs to Messiah – it always has and it always will. Faith knows that.

A faith that would fulfil the desires of Jesus John 17

The world/church issue featured as a factor in Jesus' prayer in which he said that he was not praying for the world, but for those his Father had given him (17:9). To these he gave eternal life (17:2), revealed the Father (17:6) and imparted the truth concerning his uniqueness (17:8), and they for their part believed that the Father had sent him.

Jesus' desires for them were quite specific: he wanted his followers to live as a joyful and united group who were committed to the things he had taught them. But to achieve this they needed to be protected from the evil one, the father of lies, who would attempt to corrupt and destroy their testimony. Jesus had guarded them and kept them safe from error up till now, but he was deliberately handing this role over to the Father (17:11,15). It was truth that gave their joy its solidity. That was why Jesus linked the concept of his joy to the things he had taught (17:13). If they believed a lie it would merely create a temporary and false peace that was the product of deception. And this would soon be exposed as empty when the day of reckoning arrived. The only valid foundation was the truth, and specifically the truth of God's message in Jesus Christ. That, after all, was why he had brought the Father's message (17:14) and it was why he prayed that his people would be separated to God in that environment of truth (17:17). In this it was vital that they were united in spirit and purpose. So Jesus prayed intensely that his people's unity would mirror the unity of the Godhead and so convince the world that he was the sent one (17:11,21-23).

****

Faith, then, starts as a welcome towards Jesus, a captivation with him, a spiritual partaking of him and a trust in him. But that is just the start.

People of faith witness its growth and strength as they adopt a lifestyle marked by humble service. They align their praying to God's will as he reveals it because they appreciate the crucial role Jesus has now both in heaven and on earth. They continue to love him in a living relationship and ongoing fellowship, and therefore are prepared to endure whatever may come by way of trial or opposition. And their settled goal in life is to live for the glory of Jesus and to fulfil God's purposes for his people that he prayed about.

This was the way ahead for his people then; and it is the way ahead for his people now.

It is the desired outcome of the good news that the Messiah brought and embodied.

Lightning Source UK Ltd.
Milton Keynes UK
UKOW02f1854051114

241080UK00007B/166/P

9 781490 853208